TRANSLATIONS OF CHRISTIAN LITERATURE
SERIES III
LITURGICAL TEXTS

THE PILGRIMAGE OF ETHERIA

THE PILGRIMAGE OF ETHERIA

By M. L. MC CLURE
and C. L. FELTOE, D.D.

WIPF & STOCK · Eugene, Oregon

Wipf and Stock Publishers
199 W 8th Ave, Suite 3
Eugene, OR 97401

The Pilgrimage of Etheria
Translations of Christian Literature,
Series III, Liturgical Texts
By McClure, M. L. and Feltoe, Charles Lett
Softcover ISBN-13: 978-1-6667-6367-6
Hardcover ISBN-13: 978-1-6667-6368-3
eBook ISBN-13: 978-1-6667-6369-0
Publication date 11/1/2022
Previously published by SPCK, 1919

This edition is a scanned facsimile of
the original edition published in 1919.

CONTENTS

	PAGE
INTRODUCTION	vii
1. THE NARRATIVE AND ITS AUTHORSHIP .	vii
2. THE PRESENT EDITION AND ITS EDITORS .	xv
3. ETHERIA'S ROUTE TO CONSTANTINOPLE .	xvii
4. RÉSUMÉ OF HER JOURNEYINGS . .	xvii
5. ECCLESIASTICAL ORGANIZATION . .	xxvi
6. THE MONKS AND NUNS SHE MET . .	xxvii
7. HER USE OF THE BIBLE . . .	xxxi
8. LIST OF BIBLE REFERENCES . . .	xxxv
9. THE LIVES OF THE SAINTS . . .	xxxvi
10. POINTS OF LITURGICAL INTEREST . .	xxxvii
11. THE CHURCHES IN JERUSALEM . .	xlv
12. LIST OF CHIEF GREEK WORDS USED . .	xlvii
TEXT	1
INDEX OF PROPER NAMES AND THINGS . . .	97

ILLUSTRATIONS

Facing page

I. THE BEGINNING OF VALERIUS'S LETTER TO THE RELIGIOUS BRETHREN vii

II. RED GRANITE GROUP OF RAMESES II. AND THE GOD ATUM 16

III. THE MOSAIC IN S. PUDENZIANA AT ROME, SAID TO BE IN PART OF THE FOURTH CENTURY . 45

THE BEGINNING OF VALERIUS'S LETTER
TO THE RELIGIOUS BRETHREN.

[Facing page vii.

The Pilgrimage of Etheria.

INTRODUCTION

1. The Narrative and its Authorship

THIS book was discovered by Signor Gamurrini in a MS. of the eleventh century at Arezzo, and he published it first in 1887 and again, in a correcter edition, in 1888. Three years later an English translation with text and notes, by Dr. J. H. Bernard, and an appendix on the topography by Sir C. W. Wilson, appeared under the auspices of the Palestine Pilgrims Text Society. In 1895 Dom Cabrol issued a treatise of some importance entitled *Les Églises de Jérusalem.* Then came M. Paul Geyer's edition in 1898 in vol. xxxix. of the Vienna *Corpus Script. Eccl Lat.*, who still further emended and elucidated the text. Up till that time Signor Gamurrini's conjecture that the authoress was Silvia of Aquitaine, sister of the Emperor Theodosius's minister Rufinus had been considered plausible, but had not been either corroborated or disproved.[1] But in 1903 Dom Férotin (*Revue des questions historiques*, vol. lxxiv.) sought to identify her with the virgin named Etheria, mentioned

[1] Another conjecture was put forward by Köhler (*Bibliothèque des chartes*, xlv. p. 141 ff.) in 1884 that she was Galla Placidia, daughter of Theodosius, who is said to have visited Jerusalem from Constantinople about 423 ; but this pilgrimage rests on an untrustworthy tradition, and the conjecture has never met with much acceptance from others.

by Valerius in a letter to the religious brethren of the Vierzo in N.-W. Spain, and his arguments have met with very general acceptance. In 1909, however, a detailed and determined attack upon his views was made by Karl Meister in the *Rheinisches Museum*, so far as the date and nationality of the pilgrim are concerned ; but his arguments were in Monseigneur Duchesne's opinion [1] successfully met and answered by the Abbé Deconinck (*Revue Biblique*, 1910) and others. No one probably now adheres to the theory that Silvia was the pilgrim. Meister himself agrees with the other scholars already mentioned who have identified her with the abbess named Etheria,[2] to whom Valerius refers ; he only disputes her date and nationality.

Dom Férotin's theory, amounting almost to a certainty, was that she was a fellow-countrywoman of Valerius, who had visited the East towards the end of the fourth century, *i. e.* in the reign of Theodosius († 395). Valerius himself lived in the second half of the seventh century, and is chiefly known as the biographer of his contemporary S. Fructuosus, bishop of Braga. He was abbat of the *monasterium Rufianense*, near Astorga, in the mountainous district of Gallaecia, now called the Vierzo. In the letter mentioned above he speaks of Etheria as *extremo occidui maris Oceani littore exorta* (sprung from the farthest shore of the western sea, the Ocean), chap. iv, while a doubtful phrase, where the true

---

[1] See his *Christian Worship*, p. 541 : S.P.C.K.
[2] It may, however, be mentioned that *Eucheria* or *Egeria* has been suggested as the correct form of the name, but Duchesne still (1918) definitely pronounces in favour of Etheria.

INTRODUCTION ix

reading is uncertain, in chap. i., seems, nevertheless, almost necessarily to connect Etheria with the *extremitas huius occiduae plagae* (the farthest part of this western coast). If *huius* occurred in the first of these two expressions, the inference that she was from Gallaecia would be certain : as it is, the phrases are so similar that very little doubt can be entertained that she was.[1]

Meister, however, maintains that they do not of necessity indicate this district, and that, *inter alia*, as her language exhibits no trace of the Spanish dialect, but distinct traces of that of *Gallia Narbonensis*, and as she refers to the river Rhone (on p. 31) as if it were familiar both to herself and her readers,[2] she came from S.-E. Gaul,[3] and that her monastery was perhaps at Marseilles or Arles, where there were well-known religious houses in the sixth century, to which he assigns her pilgrimage, viz. in the first half of the reign of Justinian († 565).

A considerable portion of Meister's argument rests upon the language used by Etheria. He goes into minute details over her usages, and the upshot of his examination is that she was not unlearned, but was familiar with the Scriptures, to the language of which

[1] We may compare the bishop of Edessa's remark (p. 42), that she had taken the trouble to come *de extremis porro terris*.

[2] This is practically the only reference to European topography in the extant portions of the narrative, and certainly implies acquaintance with the Rhone, but can hardly outweigh the expressions of Valerius quoted. It is not unlikely that she crossed the Rhone at some point in her journey to the East.

[3] These were among the arguments which had weighed with the earlier editors, who sought to identify the pilgrim with S. Silvia of Aquitaine.

her own is similar, her phrases being often suggested by, or formed from, the same : this seems to him to point to a later date and a different nationality [1] than the one we have accepted. We, too, do not think she was for her time and country badly educated and unlearned nor unfamiliar with the Scriptures : no one could think that. But, making all possible allowances for the inaccuracies of the scribe [2] to whom we owe our knowledge of her narrative—and they are probably serious and frequent—yet the fact remains that she wrote a very slipshod Latin : her deficiencies cannot all be due to the carelessness or ignorance of the copyist. And this is the more surprising because, though she does not appear to have picked up any Syriac or other native tongue in her journeys, yet she is by no means without knowledge of Greek : for she uses quite a large number of Greek words and phrases [3] and transliterates them as a rule with accuracy. (See list on p. xlviii f.) Besides that she displays great intelligence and exercises great powers of observation and appreciation of what she sees and hears wherever she goes. And this makes her narrative always lively

[1] Dom Férotin has also gone briefly into the question of language in footnote 2 on pp. 26 f., and comes to the conclusion that there are several definite traces of the *Spanish* dialect. This serves to show how risky such investigations and conclusions usually are!
[2] Gamurrini held that he belonged to the great Benedictine house of Monte Cassino in the eleventh century.
[3] Mrs. McClure has given two examples out of many in her note on p. 10, where Etheria's titles for her sisters find interesting parallels in the Greek and Coptic Ostraca and Letters, as published in Crum's *Coptic Ostraca* and Hall's *Coptic and Greek Texts*, but no great stress can be laid on that point, as similar forms of address are not infrequent in Patristic writings generally.

INTRODUCTION

and entertaining in spite of the defects in her style and occasional obscurity of meaning.

Stress has been laid, and not without reason, on the indications of Etheria's social importance which her story affords.[1] Wherever she went, she was well received and entertained by bishops, clergy and monks, who spared no pains in acting as ciceroni to her. She was provided with escorts of Roman soldiers when passing through a disturbed and dangerous district between Sinai and Egypt (p. 14), but dispensed with their services when it was no longer necessary to trouble them (p. 17). Though she often uses the first person singular as the head of the pilgrimage, yet she no less often speaks of "we" and "us" in a way which serves to show that she travelled with a certain retinue of her own; while, in the journey to Mount Sinai, she was also accompanied by certain holy guides (*deductores*), and again when she went to Mount Nebo. The cost of this expedition from West to East and back again, which occupied several years,[2] must have been great, however abundant the hospitality was which she met with. In the return from Mount Sinai to Clysma (Suez) she mentions the "animals" she used: these were apparently

---

[1] Valerius only calls her *beatissima sanctimonialis* (nun), but three times in the (thirteenth century) catalogues of S. Martial of Limoges she is called *abbatissa* (Férotin, p. 33). Férotin (p. 29) also draws attention to the coincidence, if it be nothing more, that the Emperor Theodosius was from Gallaecia and removed his family to Constantinople about the time of Etheria's pilgrimage; this may have considerably helped to gain her a welcome in the East, if she was in any way connected with the Court.

[2] See her statements on pp. 30 and 43 f. Cf. Valerius, chap. i. *per multa annorum spatia*.

INTRODUCTION

not camels, for she immediately speaks of them by name as used by the natives of Paran; but for the first part of the ascent of Mount Nebo (east of Jordan) she was able to use *asellus* (an ass or mule), whereas she had to walk all the way up Mount Sinai, not even a *sella* (litter) being possible because of its great steepness. If she had been an ordinary pilgrim in those days she would have been content to go on foot the whole way.[1] Such considerations again were amongst those which led earlier editors to identify our pilgrim, as has been said above, with either Galla Placidia or with Silvia of Aquitaine. But though there is a certain amount in Silvia's case that fits in with what is here contained, yet the terms in which the *Lausiac History of Palladius*[2] speaks of her in connexion with her journey from Jerusalem to Egypt show that she was an ascetic of the most severe type in her practices, and that our pilgrim never shows herself to have been, however much she respects and admires asceticism in those she meets or visits.

Three other matters remain to be considered which bear upon the date of the narrative besides being of general interest:—

(*a*) Etheria speaks of the three bishops whom she

---

[1] Valerius, chap. i. says *paulisper duce Domino gradiendo pervenit ad sacralissima loca*, and chap. v. *in hac vita pedibus peregrinavit*, but these may be only conventional phrases of his for a pilgrimage. No stress can be laid either on Etheria's occasional use of *ambulare* (walk) to describe her movements, because it means any kind of movement, e.g. *ambulare cum camelis suis*, p. 12, etc.

[2] Chap. lv.: she was sixty years of age, never used water (except for the tips of her fingers before communicating), never slept on a bed nor travelled in a litter. This is her own account of herself!

INTRODUCTION

came across in Mesopotamia (at Bathnae, Edessa and Haran) as conspicuous for their holiness, "being both monk and confessor" in each case. She does not apply this word "confessor" to any other of the bishops, although she has several times noted that they were or had been monks formerly, while the still vigorous old priest whom she saw on Mount Sinai had been "both a monk from an early age and, as they say here, an ascete."[1] According to Monseigneur Duchesne, "we know that" the three bishops who are called confessors "were victims of the persecution under Valens" (A.D. 367–378), (p. 547). We can hardly be said to "know" this, but only that this is more likely that they were, other things being considered, than that they were those whom the Emperor Anastasius, favouring the Monophysites, drove out in the early years of the sixth century (as Meister maintains). Is it, however, altogether certain that "confessor" in these three cases means more than a stricter ascete than an ordinary monachus? Duchesne himself recognizes that this is a frequent meaning of the title in those days (see *Christian Worship*, pp. 142, 173, 284 and 420; and Batiffol, *Hist. du Brév. Rom.*, p. 57). Still Eulogius, bishop of Edessa († 388), seems to have suffered persecution, and this would no doubt fit in with our date for the pilgrimage.

(*b*) Etheria quotes the bishop of Haran's statement to her that at that time the Persians held the district of Nisibis and Ur, and the Romans had no place

---

[1] The *sanctus monachus vir ascitis* at Carneas was apparently a strict hermit living alone in the desert; the ascetics, whose exploits she claims to have described on p. 39, are further characterized as *maiores*,

there (p. 39). As the Emperor Jovian had yielded the district to King Sapor in 363, that seems to be the explanation of the statement.[1] On the other hand, in the years 540–545 the Romans (under Belisarius) regained their supremacy in the East, so that Meister allows that the pilgrimage must have taken place before then. For that reason, among others, he assigns it to 534, or thereabouts.

(*c*) Dr. Bernard has drawn our attention to another point in favour of the earlier date, which Meister seems to have overlooked. It is this. When we come to the pilgrimages which are admittedly of the sixth century, *e.g.* the so-called *Breviarium*, and the pilgrimage of Theodosius (both of which may be dated about 530), we find among the churches in Jerusalem visited by pilgrims "S. Peter in the house of Caiaphas," and "S. Sophia in the Praetorium." Etheria knows nothing of these; she names only the Martyrium, the Anastasis, and the Church of Sion, and as her description of the holy city is rich in detail, it may be reasonably concluded that these were the only churches which she saw, and that her visit was prior to the erection of those named by Theodosius. Meister uses a similar argument to prove that the pilgrimage must be prior to the building by Justinian of the Church of S. Mary Deipara in 543 (as it certainly was); but his reasoning is equally conclusive to establish its priority to the *Breviarium* and the *Peregrinatio Theodosii*.

---

[1] It may be further noted that she had found (Roman) "soldiery with their tribune" stationed at Edessa (p. 32).

2. THE PRESENT EDITION AND ITS EDITORS

That part of the text, which relates to Jerusalem, had been translated for the English version (2nd edition) of Duchesne's *Origines du culte Chrétien*, which Mrs. McClure published in 1904. For it she was "mainly indebted," as she tells us, to her "brother the Rev. George Herbert, who had the advantage of many criticisms and suggestions from so eminent a scholar as the late Canon Chas. Evans, formerly Headmaster of King Edward's School, Birmingham." Mr. Herbert also translated the rest of the text which now appears with the same assistance. Moreover, he read through K. Meister's book on the subject and made a careful résumé of his conclusions for her, of which use has been freely made in this Introduction. Most of the footnotes were added to the text by Mrs. McClure herself, a few by the present writer. But, though the results of their joint labours had been set up in print for some time and she had spent a good deal of time in further research and thought over them with a view to writing the Introduction, she had to lay the work aside while she was completing the fifth edition of *Christian Worship* and seeing it through the press. This she had hardly done, when she was called away, just as she was intending to resume her work on the Pilgrimage of Etheria last summer (1918). There are many reasons why we mourn her loss, and surely among them we must reckon this, that we are not now permitted to share with her the joy of seeing the fruits of her long study brought to completion. She left very few materials for the Introduction behind among her papers, and though the present writer has in all cases done his best to utilize what there was and to reproduce what he thought to be in her mind on various points, yet he has had very largely to start *de novo* in drawing up the introductory sections, and to treat the text more or less independently. He must be forgiven, therefore, if he has failed sometimes to do justice to her ideas and to the researches on which she had so long been engaged, and if there is a certain amount of confusion in arrangement and of discrepancy between her part of the volume and his.

Mrs. McClure had frequently discussed points with friends of considerable expert knowledge like Archbishop Bernard, Monseigneur Duchesne, Professor Flinders Petrie, and others, and sometimes mentions them by name in her notes as having told her this or that. The first named of these had written a short "Foreword" to the volume in September 1916, but he has requested the present writer to withdraw it as being no longer suitable to its purpose, and to use the additional facts that he there gave in his own Introduction. This he has been very glad to do, and begs to acknowledge his indebtedness to his Grace for them, as well as to others who have contributed to the production of the book in its present form, and in particular to the Rev. A. D. Rigby, who has read through the proofs and made several valuable suggestions, which he has been able to adopt.

3. ETHERIA'S ROUTE (TO AND FROM CONSTANTINOPLE)

We have, of course, no hint of the route taken by Etheria from her home in the extreme west of Europe as far as Constantinople and back again, unless her mention of the river Rhone be taken as indicating that she crossed it in her journey (possibly at Arles).[1] But it is interesting to note that, nearly fifty years before her, the anonymous "Pilgrim of Bordeaux" gives the route which she pursued, and that may possibly have been Etheria's too. She went out by land, she tells us, across the north of Italy, through Noricum, Pannonia, Moesia, Dacia and Thrace; while on her return she embarked at Aulon in Epirus and crossed the South Adriatic to Hydruntum (Otranto) and reached home by Rome and Milan.

4. A RÉSUMÉ OF THE JOURNEYINGS

The narrative, as we now possess it, opens in the middle of a sentence at the point where the pilgrim had already reached the megalithic remains at Kibroth Hattaavah in sight of the mountain range of Sinai. It may reasonably be assumed that the missing part contained the account of her journey from her Western home to Constantinople,[2] from

---

[1] Dom Férotin (p. 31) also suggests that another hint is the statement of Peter the Deacon (twelfth century), who made large use of her narrative in his tract *De Sanctis Locis*, that she knew the flavour of the fish caught in the Mediterranean, but surely this is a little far-fetched.

[2] For this see § 3 above.

thence through what is now Asia Minor to Antioch [1] and on to Jerusalem, the events of her stay there (apart from the description of the services which she gives later on, pp. 45 ff.) and her journey from thence towards Mount Sinai by way of Clysma (now Suez) and Faran (or Paran). She had just before probably ascended "the mountain of Faran," where the hands of Moses were uplifted during the battle with Amalek (Exod. xvii. 10 ff.), and came down again into the plain (see p. xxii below). By this time the mountains lie only four miles distant, and, passing along the wide, flat valley that lies between, they soon arrive at their foot on the western side. Sir C. W. Wilson has no doubt that the peak which she calls the Mount of God and made a point of ascending was Jebel Musa (the traditional site, 7363 ft. high), though it would actually be impossible for her to see what she was told she saw from the top (p. 6): like so many tourists she was misinformed. She went also to what she was told was Mount Horeb, where Elijah's cave was,[2] and there

---

[1] See p. 43. It is not easy to fit in her visit to Alexandria and the Thebaid: perhaps she had taken ship from Tarsus or Seleucia, the port of Antioch for Alexandria, and reached Palestine from there, or had she gone straight to that part of Egypt, when she left Jerusalem and was returning from it for her visit to Sinai when we find her where the narrative now begins? The latter alternative seems on the whole the more likely, though either of them will account for the expression used on p. 6 that "the Parthenian sea" which she was told she saw from Mount Sinai "leads to Alexandria." No doubt she called to mind her sea-trip then, and was not too critical of her guides' assertions.

[2] No doubt the site which is now shown as such. In the sixth century Jebel el Deir, a little further off, was identified with Horeb.

INTRODUCTION

she specially mentions "the very earnest prayer"[1] with which they made the oblation. Thence they descended on the eastern side to the place of the Burning Bush (where the present convent of S. Catherine is), and after visiting Taberah and several other sites she returned down the valley again to Faran, and so back after two days' rest, by a toilsome route across the desert to Clysma, where she was again glad to rest for a while.

When she had been in Egypt before, she had seen something of Goshen as well as of the Thebaid and Alexandria, but she was now desirous to explore the route of the Exodus more carefully. She found it was no easy journey of four stations across the desert to what she calls "the city of Arabia" (identified by experts with the *Thou* of Roman official documents, or possibly Bubastir), and the district was apparently at the time unsettled and in military occupation. However, she was allowed an escort of soldiers, and set out. The route lay past Epauleum (Pi-hahiroth), where there was a Roman garrison, then through two other forts, Migdol and Baal-zephon, and onwards by way of Etham, Succoth, Pithom (another fort) to Heroopolis (then only a large village), on a branch of the Nile and within the borders of Egypt. The remainder of the journey into Goshen[2] was then accomplished. It took her past Rameses, which was only four miles from her

---

[1] *orationem impensissimam*, a phrase which reminds us of the ἐκτενὴς ἱκεσία in the Liturgy of S. Chrysostom: cf. Valerius, chap. ii, *cum omni exultatione et letitia inter crebra orationum preconia salutaris Deo obtulit hostias.*

[2] Only sixteen miles according to Etheria; but it should be twenty-six according to Wilson.

goal, "the city of Arabia," which she reached on the eve of the Epiphany in time for the services. Here she sent back her military guard, as she was now on the high road from the Thebaid to Pelusium, and would have no difficulty, when she resumed her journey towards Palestine. At Rameses (Saft el Henneh), which was once a great city, she found nothing but ruins remaining except two great statues cut out of "one great Theban stone" and an ancient sycamore famous for its healing virtue, which they called "the Tree of Truth"[1] according to the "bishop of Arabia," who had come out to meet her there. His account also was that Pharaoh had burnt the place to the ground in anger at the Israelites' escape.

Etheria's route lay for two days right through the land of Goshen along the banks of the Nile, and she was greatly struck with the fertility and beauty of this district (p. 17).[2] In an article by Miss Amelia Betham Edwards, which appeared in *Harper's Magazine*, October 1886, we read the following interesting comments on this: "This was *before* the submerging of the 'field of Zoan' by lake Menzaleh. Mas'oudy, the Arab traveller and historian of the tenth century, thus describes it: 'The place occupied by the lake was formerly a district which had not its equal in

---

[1] "E. Naville in *Goshen*, pp. 12, 20, quotes inscriptions on the monuments of Saft, in which the sycomore tree is mentioned. We see that in the fourth century the tradition was yet surviving, though clothed in Christian garb" (Bernard, p. 22 *n.*). Mrs. McClure has left a note among her papers to this effect: "Certain sycomores on the verge of the desert are still venerated. The Fellahs put vases of water under them. If asked for what use, the answer is: For passers by and pigeons."

[2] Cf. Valerius, chap. i.: *singularum provinciarum magnitudines, uberrimas fertilitates atque perspicuas . . . describens.*

INTRODUCTION

Egypt for fine air, fertility and wealth. Gardens, plantations of palms and other trees, vines and cultivated fields met the eye in every direction. In short, there was not a province in Egypt except the Fayum, to be compared with it for beauty. This district was distant about one day's journey from the sea. . . . But in the year 251 of the era of Diocletian (A. D. 535) the waters of the sea flowed in and submerged that part of the plain which now is called the Lake of Tennis, and every year the inundation increased, so that at last it covered the whole province.'" We know that the late Mrs. McClure considered this an additional corroboration of her conviction that Meister's date for the pilgrimage was wrong: and it is certainly a remarkable sidelight on the narrative, if the date and the other statements are to be relied on.

Between "the city of Arabia" and Pelusium on the sea coast she mentions only one place that she passed through, viz. Tathnis, which is taken as more likely to be the ancient Tahpanhes (or Daphno)[1] than Tanis (Zoan), but the two places were not far apart, and the relevancy of the extract just given is not affected.

Without further description of her journey Etheria arrived once more in Jerusalem.

She now proceeds to describe another expedition she undertook from there, viz. to make the ascent of Mount Nebo in the land of Moab. This time she was accompanied by several of the clergy and monks. They crossed the Jordan by Jericho and, passing through Livias, came to the mountain, and having

[1] See note on p. 17.

reached the top, were much delighted with the panorama spread before them, particulars of which she gives. They then returned to the Holy City. Her next tour was through Jericho again and then northwards up the Jordan valley until they came first to Salem, where they visited Melchizedek's church and city; then to Aenon, Thisbe (Elijah's native place) and the brook Cherith, and so, crossing the Jordan, into the Ausitis (Uz), when they made the burying-place of Job at Carneas (or Dennaba) the final point in their journey. The church had been "built by some tribune," but left unfinished. Here again Etheria refers to the thankfulness and joy with which she and her companions made their communion at the special oblation, which the bishop offered at her request before they returned once more to Jerusalem.[1] But there is a gap in the MS. in the middle of the account of this tour. After leaving the brook Cherith they continued up the valley until they saw on the left towards Phœnicia (on the N.W.) "a great and very high mountain which extended," and there the gap begins, and when the story is taken up again we are at Job's burial-place. Valerius (chap. ii.), mentions several mountains as visited by her, which are omitted in our fragments: Faran, where Moses prayed with hands uplifted, but that no doubt she described before our fragments begin (p. 1); Tabor, the scene of our Lord's Transfiguration; Hermon, where the Lord was wont to rest Himself with His disciples, and the mountain where our Lord taught His disciples the beatitudes, etc. The shape of

[1] Cf. Valerius, chap. ii. : *cibo Verbi Dei refecta, infatigabiliter agens gratias Deo carpebat iter intrepida.*

INTRODUCTION

Tabor, which is conical and not very high, does not suit Etheria's description. One would think, therefore, that it was part of the Hermon range that she saw, and that by the time she saw it, she had turned east to cross the Jordan.

The time had now come for Etheria to return to her own country, but still full of energy and desire to see as much as she could, she determined to make a big detour from Antioch, which would lie in her direct course by land to Constantinople, and visit from there several important and interesting places in N.-W. Syria and Mesopotamia before turning her face westwards. Accordingly, when she left Antioch she went first to Hierapolis, and from there reached the great river Euphrates, which she can only compare with the Rhone for its width and strong current. They crossed it in a ship and came to Bathnae (in Osrhoene), and from thence arrived at Edessa, the chief goal of her desires, where she stayed three days and had a busy and very interesting time. Matters of interest are involved in this portion of the narrative, which deserve attention.

Etheria expressly says she went to Edessa to pray at the martyrium of S. Thomas the Apostle, whose whole body is there. And when she arrived there, she and her companions went at once to the church and the martyrium of S. Thomas. She found the great and beautiful church had been rebuilt in a new form (*nova compositione*). This the Emperor Valens had finished in 372 (Socr., *Hist. Eccl.* iv. 18). Her language seems, though not at all certainly, to imply that the martyrium was still separate from the church. The Chronicle of Edessa says the tomb was transferred to the new church in 394, when Cyrus was bishop, who had succeeded Eulogius on his death in 388. This again seems to corroborate the date we have accepted for her pilgrimage.

She visited many other martyria in the town, but makes no specific allusion to the famous likeness of our Lord, though it is said to have been held in veneration at least as early as the middle of the fourth century.

She does, however, describe two other striking likenesses which she was taken to see, though that can hardly be more than a coincidence—viz. the marble busts or images (*archiotepa*) of King Abgar and his son Magnus [1] in the royal palace (p. 33).

Etheria gives us likewise an account that will be read with interest of what she was told about the letters of Abgar to our Lord and His answer. This account differs from that of Eusebius (*Hist. Eccl.* ii. 13), in mentioning the promise of Christ that no enemy should ever enter the city. Eusebius knows nothing of such a promise of immunity, though later historians relate it (see Bernard's note, p. 36), and it was known to Ephraem Syrus (about 390). She also mentions that she had copies of these letters at home. Meister points out that Rufinus's translation of Eus. *Hist. Eccl.* into Latin was not complete before 398 at the earliest, from which he argues that copies would not be known in the West so soon as the date assigned by Gamurrini and adopted by ourselves. But there may have been other sources or authorities, Greek as well as Latin, besides Eusebius; nor was Etheria,

[1] According to Smith, *Dict. of Christian Biog.*, *s.v.* Abgar, several Edessene princes bore the name Ma'nû.

INTRODUCTION xxv

perhaps, quite so ignorant of Greek as is usually thought, and her copies may have been in that language after all.

From Edessa she went on to Haran and stayed there two days, one of them being April 24, the festival of S. Helpidius (see note on p. 37).[1] She would very much have liked to penetrate farther east to Nisibis, and then on to Ur of the Chaldees ; but the bishop dissuaded her on the ground that that district was now in the hands of the Persians, no longer the Romans (see p. 39). She was content, therefore, to go only six miles out and see the well from which Jacob watered Rachel's flocks, at a place called Fadana (the Paddan-Aram of Gen. xxviii. 2). She then returned to Antioch and pursued her westward journey, through Cilicia, till she came to Tarsus. Here she made another detour by way of Pompeiopolis (or Soli) and Corycus (both on the sea coast), in order to pay a special visit to the tomb of S. Thecla in Isauria, where she met to her great delight her dear friend Marthana, whom she had known in Jerusalem (see note on p. xxix). Coming back to Tarsus she made her way without further delay by Mopsocrene (which she calls Mansocrenae) and under Mount Taurus through Cappadocia, Galatia and Bithynia, until she arrived at Chalcedon, and stopped there for the famous shrine of S. Euphemia, and finally arrived at Constantinople.[2] There she visited

[1] The ascete of this name described by Palladius (*Laus. Hist.* chap. xlviii.) is apparently a different person.

[2] She had taken the same route along the great Roman high road on her way out from Constantinople, more than three years before, and on that occasion also had come to know the shrine of S. Euphemia (p. 43).

the Church of the Apostles (p. 44) and many other of the martyria with which the city abounded: and, still indefatigable, tells her beloved sisters that, while she is preparing this narrative for them there and also, it seems, drawing up her account of the services and rites which she had witnessed at Jerusalem, she will not actually leave for home till she has crossed into Asia once again and visited the martyrium of S. John at Ephesus. If anything further remains to tell and her life is spared, she will relate it in person or in another letter. And so she brings her story to an end, which investigation proves to be as veracious as it is undoubtedly vivacious throughout.[1]

5. THE ECCLESIASTICAL ORGANIZATION

Etheria practically gives no description and makes no comment on the Church organization of the districts through which she journeyed, except that she mentions (1) the bishops and other clergy whom she met, often saying that they had been, or still were, from among the ranks of the monastic orders, and (2) the churches in which they ministered. At the end of the fourth century Egypt was an independent province under the Patriarch of Alexandria, but the part of Egypt she mostly mentions would hardly have been organized by that time into what afterwards became known as Augustanica Prima, with fourteen bishops, the chief of whom was at Pelusium. The

[1] Valerius's characteristic summary, for all its loose grammar and rhetorical exaggeration, is worth quoting: *totius mundi itinera non quassabat, maria procellosa ac flumina ingentia non conclusit, montium immanitas diraque asperitas non imminuit, gentium imbiarum truculentissima atrocitas non perterruit* (chap. iii.).

INTRODUCTION xxvii

bishop of Jerusalem had had special privileges granted him at the Council of Nicæa (325), but he was still "under the jurisdiction of his provincial metropolitan, the Bishop of Cæsarea" (Duchesne, *op. cit.*, p. 27) : and therefore probably the clergy west of the Jordan she had to do with outside the Holy City were likewise dependent on the latter. To the east and north-east of the Jordan as far as Hierapolis (p. 31) the places she visited were probably all in the domain of the Patriarch of Antioch, while those in Mesopotamia would be under the Catholicos of Armenia.

6. THE MONKS AND NUNS OF THE NARRATIVE

It is a matter of common knowledge that monasticism took its rise in Egypt about the middle of the third century, perhaps as the result of the Decian persecution, many of those who then fled to the desert never returning, and that from the beginning of the fourth century the movement developed mainly along two lines which were almost contemporaneous[1] : (1) under the method of S. Antony, whose monks were mostly solitary hermits in the strict sense, though in some places they lived near one another in small companies and met together for common worship on Saturdays and Sundays : (2) under the rule of S. Pachomius, who founded the conventual type of monasticism. Here the brethren lived together in much larger bands, and not only combined for common

[1] The monks of Nitria and Scete, to the south of Alexandria, would more or less represent a third (see Lowther Clarke, *S. Basil*, p. 33), and Etheria may have come across them when she was at Alexandria (p. 18).

INTRODUCTION

worship but were organized for regular work (on the land, etc.), though they took no meals together and were each allowed to practise that amount of austerity which his strength and zeal prompted beyond the fixed minimum which was obligatory on all.[1] Thus the spirit of individualism was a strongly marked feature in both these systems. It was from Egypt by way of Rome that monasticism was quite early brought to western Europe, and there for some time it retained many of its more especially Eastern characteristics. The community of feeling and atmosphere, therefore, between the monastic institutions of the West and those of Egypt, Syria and Palestine was considerable, and will account for the readiness with which Etheria was received everywhere on her journeys and for the highly appreciative way in which she commends the saintliness of her entertainers and informants, who were in the greater number of instances closely associated with the monastic and ascetic life.

The rule of S. Pachomius, which sprang into a full organization almost at once (like Minerva from the head of Jove), spread rapidly, but into Palestine the monastic life was introduced early in the fourth century, not by him, but by a disciple of S. Antony, Hilarion. There "the original impulse to the eremitic life survived, and the cenobitic ideal made little headway either now or later. In Syria and Mesopotamia asceticism was, so to speak, indigenous."[2]

---

[1] See what Etheria herself says on this point in connexion with the Lenten fast (pp. 61 f.).

[2] Lowther Clarke, *S. Basil*, p. 41. I am indebted for my information throughout this section to him and to Mrs. McClure's

INTRODUCTION

Consequently most if not all the monks and nuns that Etheria met in Palestine, Syria and Mesopotamia were probably either of the strictly eremitic or semi-eremitic kind (see *e.g.* p. 37).

The names she uses to describe these monks (and nuns) are various. In the former part of the narrative her regular name for them is *monachi*. We have already mentioned (p. xiii) the three instances, where she also brings in the word *ascitis* (ἀσκητής) and the three doubtful instances of the use of the word "confessor" in connexion with monks. The *ascitis* whom she heard of or met at Carneas on the east of Jordan was evidently a solitary, and so probably was the priest on Mount Sinai: also the *monachus* at Thisbe, it would seem (p. 28). A number of them came into Haran from the Mesopotamia desert on the Feast of S. Helpidius (April 24). At Seleucia in Isauria we read for the first time of women (*virgines*) as well as men, the former under the direction of a deaconess named Marthana[1] (see p. 42) whom she had previously met at Jerusalem: and also there she first uses the term *apotactitae* (ἀποτακτιταί), which for her includes members of both sexes. This term recurs several times at Jerusalem, where *monazontes* (μονάζοντες) and *parthenae* (παρθένοι) are likewise

---

extracts from Gasquet, *English Monastic Life*, who in turn frequently quotes Dom Butler's masterly introduction to the *Lausiac History of Palladius*.

[1] She is mentioned as a worthy follower of S. Thecla by the pseudo-Basil of Seleucia. According to Theodoret, *Relig. Hist.* c. 29, SS. Marana and Cyra visited both Jerusalem and S. Thecla's tomb early in the fifth century, but, if the date we have adopted for Etheria's pilgrimage is correct, the close similarity of the two names is a mere coincidence.

mentioned.[1] *Monazontes* should strictly denote "solitaries," but so should *monachi*: probably neither have always their strict significance in Etheria's vocabulary. The term *apotactitae* seems to have been an unusual one for Christian ascetics. Palladius in his *Lausiac History* frequently uses the verb ἀποτάξασθαι of those who renounced the pleasures and pursuits of the world, and Cassian gave his book the title of *de institutis renuntiantium*, where *renuntiantes* bears the same sense, but otherwise *apotactites* was one of the names assumed by such ascetic heretics as the Manichaean *Encratites*, etc.[2] Evidently, however, in Etheria's usage it is more or less equivalent to *monachi* (*monazontes*) and *parthenae* (*virgines*) and has not the least sinister association.

One other word, which is connected with this subject, needs a little explanation. Etheria constantly speaks of the monks' *monasteria*. It follows from what has been said that with her in the singular *monasterium* means a cell, mostly that of a solitary, and in the plural *monasteria* means a collection of cells, where monks were living under semi-eremetic conditions, more probably under the method of S. Anthony than under the rule of S. Pachomius. Thus the aged priest on Mount Sinai came out *de monasterio suo* (p. 4), and the bishop of "the city of Arabia," whom she had known ever since she was in the Thebaid, had been brought up *a pisinno* (from his boyhood) *in monasterio*. [This man, in passing, is

---

[1] She there also refers to *laici* (p. 45) and *saeculares* (p. 96) as distinguished from *clerici*.

[2] Cf. Epiph., *Haer.* lxi. 506-513. They were condemned by edicts of Theodosius in 381 and 383 (Bernard, p. 43).

quite worthy of further notice, because Etheria tells us that " in consequence he was both well learned [1] in the scriptures and chastened in his whole life," besides being " courteous and most kind in receiving pilgrims" —truly a charming picture of an old-world church dignitary.] For instances of *monasteria* (collections of cells) we may refer to what is said of them under Mount Sinai on p. 5, where the monks' successful cultivation of the lower slopes is well described, and again to those she visited round Rachel's well near Haran, and the *monasteria sine numero virorum ac mulierum* which she found surrounding the church at Seleucia.[2] These last were all enclosed in a high wall which had been raised to protect them from the inroads of the brigands who infested the district (p. 42).

7. Etheria's Use of the Bible

Etheria's usual name for the Bible is *Scriptura* (either in the singular or the plural, and with or without the epithet " Holy "). Twice she uses the expression " the Scriptures of God " (pp. 16 and 40). She characterizes the Pentateuch, from which she naturally quotes most often, as " the (holy) books of (holy) Moses." The most interesting of the titles she uses, however, is (on p. 38) *scriptura canonis* (" the Scripture of the Canon "), a title which is apparently almost unknown otherwise. Westcott (*Canon of*

[1] She says the same thing of the bishop of Haran (p. 38).
[2] Valerius (chap. i.) uses two different words in describing Etheria's visit to the Thebaid, viz. *visitans monachorum . . . congregationum cenobia, similiter et . . . anachoretarum ergastula*, but has no special reference to the conditions of living she found among the monks in other parts.

N. T. pp. 504 f.) doubted whether Credner's term γραφαὶ κανόνος had any justification. He himself quoted from Amphilochius (*circ.* 380) the following as the nearest approach to it:—

οὗτος ἀψευδέστατος
κανὼν ἂν εἴη τῶν θεοπνεύστων γραφῶν.

But now Etheria (*ex hypothesi* this writer's contemporary) has given us an even more exact equivalent. As Bishop Westcott says, *Canon* here must mean the authoritative rule or standard, by which the books have been ratified and approved in the Church.

Her quotations and references to the books of the Old Testament usually give a close representation of the Greek of the Septuagint, although we may imagine from her imperfect knowledge of Greek that they are based on a pre-Vulgate Latin version, not on the Septuagint itself. The proper names she quotes are, as we have shown in the text, good instances of this, and to these we may add one which is perhaps the clearest of all: on p. 26 her *Quodollagomor* (cf. Gen. xiv.) represents almost exactly the LXX Χοδολλογόμορ, while our Eng. Chedorlaomer represents the Vulg. Chodorlahomor. She has, however, made a slip in calling him "king of Nations" instead of king of Elam: see note *in loco*. There are a few variations or divergencies which are worthy of note, though it is, of course, doubtful how far they are due to carelessness in her own or her copyist's transcription. The principal of these are as follows:—

(1) pp. 8 f. Exod. iii. 5, *corrigiam calceamenti* (the

latchet of thy shoe). Here the LXX only gives ὑπόδημα, but see Gen. xiv. 23, and S. Mark i. 7, which probably account for her version. The same reading is found in Origen (Lat. works).

(2) p. 9. Exod. xxxii. 27, *de porta in porta*. Here we should no doubt read *in portam* (LXX, ἐπὶ πύλην), as the abl. makes no sense.

(3) p. 15. Gen. xlvii. 6. Etheria's rendering here represents exactly neither the LXX text nor the Vulg., which are different from one another: she gives *in meliori terra Egypti*, where the LXX has ἐν τῇ βελτίστῃ γῇ (Vulg. *in optimo loco*), and she adds *in terra Iessen, in terra Arabiae*, which the LXX omits, while the Vulg. reads *et trade eis terram Gessen*. Probably Etheria's is meant to be only a loose paraphrase, not an exact transcription.

(4) and (5), pp. 18 and 19. For the readings and the explanations of them in Deut. xxxii. 49, and xxxiv. 8, see notes *in loco*.

(6) p. 13. In quoting apparently Numb. x. 12, and xxxiii. 36, she gives this rendering *filii Israel . . . ambulaverunt iter suum* to the LXX ἐξῆραν and ἀπῆραν (Vulg. *profecti*), but she is probably thinking rather of such phrases as πορεύεσθαι or ποιεῖσθαι ὁδόν than of the exact original: *e.g.* Prov. ii. 20, ἐπορεύοντο (Vulg. *ambulas*) τρίβους ἀγαθάς, iii. 23, ἵνα πορεύῃ (Vulg. *ambulabis*) . . . τὰς ὁδούς σου, and Judges xvii. 8, τοῦ ποιῆσαι ὁδόν.

(7) p. 6. She follows the LXX version of 1 Kings xix. 9, τί σὺ ἐνταῦθα; (*quid tu hic?*), a reading which is found in Tert. *de Jeiun.* 6.

(8) p. 36. In Gen. xxiv. 20, Etheria takes it for granted, as usual, that Abraham's "eldest servant"

is the same as Eliezer of Damascus (xv. 20), though it is merely an assumption. Again, on p. 25, it appears that she accepted the identification of the Salem of Melchizedek (Gen. xiv. 18) with the place of that name near Sychar, not as others do with Jerusalem (cf. *Jerome ad Evang.* § 27, and *Onom.*). Her statement on p. 32 that Batanis (Batnae) is mentioned in the Bible is, so far as we know, without foundation:[1] also that Moses was born at Taphnis or Tatnis (p. 17), and wrote the book of Deuteronomy in the plains of Moab (p. 19).

Her actual quotations from the New Testament are not very numerous, and the following are the only ones that need to be commented on:—

(1) In S. Mark xiv. 38 (p. 72), she omits "and pray" and renders ἵνα μή by *ne* (Vulg. *ut non*). (2) In S. Luke xxii. 41 (p. 71), καὶ αὐτὸς ἀπεσπάσθη . . . ὡσεὶ λίθου βολὴν . . . καὶ προσηύχετο, she has *et accessit . . . quantum iactus lapidis et oravit* (Vulg. *et ipse avulsus est . . . quantum iactus est lapidis . . . et orabat*). Is not *accessit* the copyist's mistake for *abscessit*? If so, it is probably a genuine reading of the Latin version Etheria used. (3) In S. John xx. 25 (p. 83), she has *non credo, nisi videro*, but the Greek is ἐὰν μὴ ἴδω . . . οὐ μὴ πιστεύσω : no doubt it is a brief paraphrase, not a quotation. (4) In her reference to S. John xix. 30, on p. 77, she uses the words *reddidit spiritum* to represent παρέδωκεν τὸ πνεῦμα, a much more expressive phrase than the Vulg. *tradidit spiritum*. Was this again the reading of her Latin text?

[1] Mr. Rigby suggests that perhaps she has confused it with Batanaea = Bashan (mod. Arab. 'Bathaniyeh'), which is not unlikely.

8. List of Biblical Quotations and References

† These passages have been commented on in the preceding pages.

	PAGE		PAGE
Gen. xi. 28	39	†Numb. x. 12	13
xi. 31	38	xi. 2 f.	10
xii. 1 (∥ Acts vii. 3)	36	xi. 25	10
xii. 4 (LXX)	36	xi. 34 (LXX)	1, 11
xiv. 1 (LXX)	26	xiii. 22 (?)	17
†xiv. 2 (LXX)	23	xx. 11	21
xiv. 8, 18	25	xxi. 26 (LXX)	23
xv. 18	31	xxi. 33 (LXX)	24
xix. 23 ff.	23	xxiii. 14 (LXX)	24
xxiv. 10, 15	38	xxiii. 28 (LXX)	24
xxiv. 15	36	xxxii. 36	19
xxviii. 2	41	†xxxiii. 36	13
xxix. 1, 2, 4	39	Deut. iii. 10 (LXX)	24
xxix. 10	40	iv. 46 (LXX)	23 f.
xxxi. 19	41	xxxi. 30 (LXX)	20
xxxiii. 11	5n.	†xxxii. 49 f. (LXX)	18
xxxvi. 32	25	xxxiii.	20
xlvi. 29 (LXX)	15	xxxiv. 3 (LXX)	23
xlvi. 34 (LXX)	13	xxxiv. 6 (LXX)	22
†xlvii. 6	15	†xxxiv. 8 f. (LXX)	19
Exodus i. 11	15	Josh. iii. 14	19
iii. 1 ff.	2	xiii. 27	19
†iii. 5	8 f.	xxii. 10 f.	19
xii. 43 ff.	15	Judges viii. 20 (?)	28
xiii. 20 (LXX)	14	xii. 7 (?)	28
xiv. 2 (LXX)	14	1 Kings xvii. 1 (LXX)	28
xiv. 10	14	xvii. 3 (LXX)	29
xvi. 13 f.	10	†xix. 9 (LXX)	6
xvii. 5	10	1 Chron. i. 43	25
xix. 18, 20	3 f.	2 Chron. vi. vii. 8 ff.	95
xxiv. 9 ff.	7	Job i. 1 (LXX)	24
xxiv. 18	2	Jerem. xliii. 7 ff.	17n.
xxxii.	2	Lam. i. 12 (LXX)	22
†xxxii. 19, 27	9		
xxxii. 20 (?)	10	S. Matt. xxi. 8 f.	52, 66
xxxiii. 22	4	xxiv. 3 f.	68
xxxiv. 4	5	xxvi. 2 ff.	73
xl. 17	11	xxvi. 14 f.	69
Numb. ix. 5	10	†S. Mark xiv. 38	72

	PAGE		PAGE
St. Mark xv. 1 ff..	73	St. John xii. 1 ff...	64
S. Luke ii. 22 ff.	56	xviii. 28 ff.	73
†xxii. 41	71	†xix. 30, 38 ff.	77
xxiii. 1 ff.	73	†xx. 19, 25	83
xxiv. 50 ff.	87	Acts i. 9 ff.	87
S. John iii. 23	27	ii. 1 ff.	36
xi. 29 f.	64	vii. 3 (‖ Gen. xii. 1)	36

9. THE LIVES OF THE SAINTS

Besides these frequent references to the Bible lessons which describe the places she visited and the actions of holy men which are there connected with them, Etheria on p. 43 mentions in set terms the Acts of S. Thecla, as having been read by her or to her, when she was at Seleucia. Her story, which is closely connected with that of S. Paul, is referred to by Tertullian, *de Bapt.* c. 17, about A.D. 200, as well as by Hilary of Poictiers and Jerome in the fourth century. The Acts of Paul and Thecla were, at one time, almost looked upon as included in the Canon.[1] At Edessa also she read besides the usual (Bible?) lessons "some things concerning S. Thomas himself" (p. 32). It is not certain what the reference here is. The well-known "Acts of Thomas" were a Gnostic document, not specially connected with Edessa nor at all likely to be used by the orthodox Etheria. The earlier legend made out that S. Thomas the Apostle sent Thaddeus to Edessa, the later version identified the two. Probably what Etheria read was either the *Doctrina Apostolorum* or the *Doctrina Addaei* or the (Greek) *Acta Thaddaei*.[2]

So, again, in connexion with what the bishop had

[1] See Smith, *Dict. of Christian Biogr.* vol. iv. p. 884.
[2] *Ibid.* vol. i. pp. 21, 31.

INTRODUCTION

quoted for her benefit at Haran (Charrae), she tells her beloved sisters that her informants were always most careful to quote from and she to listen to only the most reliable stories, whether from the scriptures themselves or from the *gesta mirabilia* of holy men (i. e. *ascetae*),[1] some of whom were dead and some still alive (p. 39).

10. Points of Liturgical Interest

1. *Epiphany*. Etheria leaves practically no room for doubt that both in Egypt and at Jerusalem the Feast of the Nativity was kept on January 6, not on December 25, and this is in accordance with what we know to be the general usage of those churches otherwise. Our Christmas Day had distinctly a Western origin, not having been introduced into the East before 375, and that was at Antioch. Juvenal, bishop of Jerusalem († 458), is said to have accepted it, but Cosmas Indicopleustes, a native of Egypt, in the first half of the sixth century, distinctly witnesses against its observance in Jerusalem then. For the vicissitudes in regard to Christmas see Duchesne, *op. cit.* pp. 259 ff., and Conybeare, *Rituale Armenorum*, p. 512.

2. The *Purification* (Feb. 14). Etheria's name for it is simply *quadragesimae de Epiphania* (the fortieth day from E.), the common name for it being Hypapante (ὑπαπαντή, or meeting, *i.e.* of the Holy Family with Simeon and Anna). This is the earliest extant

[1] These she here calls *monachi maiores*, having applied the same epithet already to the hermits, who came down from the desert hills of Mesopotamia to keep the feast of S. Helpidius and commemorate holy Abraham at Haran.

notice of it. Naturally it would begin as a favourite local commemoration in the Holy City, and thence it spread towards the West in the sixth century.

3. *Lent* at Jerusalem lasted eight weeks when Etheria was there, the forty days (or more strictly forty-one days) being made up by omitting all the eight Sundays and all the Saturdays except Easter Eve. This prolongation of the season is not mentioned elsewhere.[1] But it may be noted that the retention of the Saturday as a festival (not in Lent only) was long general in the East, if not to some extent in the West. Etheria says that in Jerusalem they call *Quadragesimae Eortae* (*i.e.* ἑορταί, feasts), but this is probably a mistake on her part due to her imperfect knowledge of Greek, ἑορτή (sing.) being commonly used for the great yearly festival of Easter.

4. The observances of *Holy Week* are all of great interest in view of the early date of the record. They included the following :—

    (*a*) The children's waving of olive or palm branches on the Sunday. This, again, started at Jerusalem.

    (*b*) The celebration of the Communion in the late afternoon of Maundy Thursday: for this practice see further below on p. xiii.

    (*c*) The adoration of the Cross and the observance of the Three Hours on Good Friday.

    (*d*) King Solomon's ring and the ancient anointing horn of the kings were also exhibited and venerated.

5. *Ascension Day* itself was kept, but without much ceremonial, and at Bethlehem, not in the Imbomon,

[1] See Bernard, p. 52, and Duchesne, p. 243.

as one would have expected. Curiously enough, however, on the afternoon of Pentecost (p. 87) meetings were held both in the Eleona and in the Imbomon at which the feast of the Ascension was again commemorated.[1]

6. The following were the *Daily Offices* :—

(a) *Vigiliae nocturnae* before dawn.
(b) *Mattins* (at dawn).
(c) *Terce* (only in Lent).
(d) *Sext*.
(e) *None*.
(f) *Lucernare* (Vespers).

No mention is made of Prime or Compline. These services were open to all who wished to attend, but naturally the chief part of the congregation consisted of ascetics of both sexes (*monazontes et parthenae*, p. 45). Three psalms [2] and three prayers were said at each office, and Etheria was agreeably impressed with the (to her unfamiliar) practice of adapting Psalms, Prayers and Lessons [3] to the special teaching of the season or place.

She also speaks of "hymns" and "antiphons" being used. The practice of "singing or saying" hymns other than the Psalms of David in Divine service was of very early origin, certainly in the East, and almost as certainly in the West; so that in any case Etheria would not have been entirely

[1] Is it possible that this portion of the narrative has been dislocated, or that Etheria herself has blundered here? But see Conybeare, *Rituale Armenorum*, p. 509.

[2] Cf. Cassian, *Inst*. 3. 3.

[3] The use of "Proper" Psalms, etc., is said not to have been introduced into the Gallican Church before the middle of the fifth century (Bernard).

INTRODUCTION

unaccustomed to it. But in the fourth century—largely in consequence of the efforts of the orthodox or catholics to counteract the spread of Arian views by this means—hymn-writing and singing had received a very great impetus, and such compositions, whether metrical (as in the West) or merely rhythmical (as in the East), had become a regular part of public worship throughout Christendom. Thus, at Constantinople we know that S. Chrysostom had encouraged their use, and at Milan S. Ambrose had himself written hymns for the purpose,[1] while at Edessa the famous Syriac hymns of Ephraem belong to about the same period, and were intended as a counterblast to the unsound teaching conveyed by the older songs of Bardesanes. With regard to the "antiphons" which Etheria mentions, it is difficult to say whether she means compositions strictly so called, because they were sung antiphonally, or in a more general sense "anthems" as we call them, for both kinds were already probably in use.[2]

It is not necessary to repeat here what Mrs. McClure has said in her footnote on p. 46 by way of possible explanation of the obscure expression "to approach the bishop's hand," which occurs frequently in Etheria's account of the services at Jerusalem.

With regard to Etheria's use of the word *missa* in her narrative, it must be remembered that it still has for her its original meaning of "dismissal," and is so

[1] The poems of Prudentius (a Spaniard) were not used as church hymns till somewhat later (in the fifth century).
[2] See *Dict. of Christian Antiq.*, *s.v.*; and for much further information on this subject as a whole the article on "Hymns in the same Dictionary, and on "Verse-writers" in *Dict. of Christian Biog.* may be consulted.

rendered in this translation. It does not seem to have been introduced into church phraseology much before the end of the fourth century, and she herself does not employ it till she begins to describe the services at Jerusalem (pp. 46 ff.). There she applies it to all kinds of meetings for public worship, and much more often to the daily or occasional offices than to the Liturgy properly so called, where, however, she is careful to distinguish between the *missa catechumenorum* and the *missa fidelium*. Her usual terms for the Eucharist are *oblatio* and *offerre*, and the congregation is usually said *procedere* for its celebration.

One quite new feature of this edition, on which Mrs. McClure has spent much care, is the use that she has made in her notes of the Old Armenian Lectionary for the purpose of identifying the psalms and lections sung or said at Jerusalem during her visit. "This evidence," says Archbishop Bernard, "supplies an interesting confirmation of the accuracy of Etheria's observations as to the nature of the services at which she was present": for the frequent references in its rubrics to Jerusalem sites are shown to be genuine and to belong to an early period by the statements of more than one Armenian father in the first half of the eighth century.[1] The information will be found set out in full in Mr. Conybeare's *Rituale Armenorum*, pp. 507 ff.: it is based upon two MSS., one at Paris in the Bibliothèque National of the eighth century, the other, at Oxford in the Bodleian, of the fourteenth century, and upon the commentary of Gregory Asharuni (early eighth century).

7. *Fasting*. Various details are given, in particular

[1] See Conybeare, *Rituale Armenorum*, pp. 181 and 508.

xlii   INTRODUCTION

with regard to Wednesdays and Fridays in Lent (p. 59) and the extra strict fast of the *Apotactitae* (pp. 61 f.); but the rules are not always quite clear, owing to Etheria's use of *Missa* (dismissal) for other services than the Eucharist, as the length of the fast depends on the hour of Communion. She speaks also of the fast after Pentecost (p. 89), which as late as the tenth century was still in theory to be observed in Western Christendom (see Dowden, *Ch. Year and Kalendar*, pp. 85 f.). We find references to it in S. Athanasius (*Apol. de fuga*, 6) and in the *Apostolic Constitutions* (v. 20). It is perhaps more than a coincidence that one of the Ember seasons in the West was fixed by the date of Pentecost.

No relaxation was allowed on account of a martyr's festival falling on a "Station" day in Lent at Jerusalem: cf. Council of Laodicea in Phrygia (A.D. 361), c. 51.

8. The *Eucharist*. The usual liturgical hour on Saturdays and Sundays was the third (9 a.m.), but on "Station" days throughout the year the ninth (3 p.m.). Once a year, on Maundy Thursday (see above), it was even later, *i.e.* after the tenth hour (4 p.m.). This last usage is stated by Archbishop Bernard (*op. cit.* p. 61) to have been after a meal, in conformity with that of the African Church (Council of Carthage, A.D. 397, c. 29, and S. Aug. Ep. *ad Januar.* c. 7), but Etheria seems to me very distinctly to state that they took their food *after*, not before (p. 71). Otherwise during Lent the Liturgy was celebrated only on Saturdays and Sundays, and not on Wednesdays and Fridays.[1]

[1] Cf. Council of Laod. c. 49.

It is interesting to note that the language employed in service time was Greek, not Syriac, though interpretations of lessons and instructions were given in Syriac for the benefit of those who did not know Greek (p. 94).

At the Sunday Eucharist as many of the priests who were present preached as wished to, and the bishop preached last of all.[1] The posture of the preacher seems to have been that of sitting (as in the Jewish synagogue), while the congregation stood. Applause as well as other signs of emotion were often called forth by the reader or speaker (p. 94).

9. The use of *incense* is mentioned on p. 49, but apparently for fumigation before the Liturgy (or at all events the ἀναφορά itself) begins, not actually as part of the ceremonial.

10. Etheria was struck by the use of the *Kyrie eleison* as a response by the numerous choir boys standing by during the recitation of the names from the diptychs at vespers (p. 47).[2] The evidence goes to show that this formula was not introduced into the West of Christendom till the end of the fifth century. The 3rd Canon of the Council of Vaison (529) speaks of it as having reached Provence by way of Rome and Milan: probably it reached Spain somewhat later. See E. Bishop, *Liturg. Hist.* pp. 116 ff.

11. *Holy Baptism.* The course of preparation of those catechumens who became *competentes* during

---

[1] See pp. 51, 56, and 85. Cf. *Apost. Const.* ii. 57.
[2] It is possible from the way in which the phrase is explained that the Latin equivalent, *Domine, miserere*, was used in her own country.

Lent and the Baptism itself on Easter Eve is fully described, and likewise the further instructions given to the newly baptized during the ensuing Eastertide. The descriptions tally in most respects with what may be gathered from S. Cyril of Jerusalem's eighteen Catechetical Lectures delivered to the *competentes* and the five on the Mysteries delivered to the neophytes in 386.

12. The *Dedication Festival:* see p. xlvi below.

13. *Martyr Memorials.* That of S. Thomas at Edessa is mentioned on p. 32; that of S. Elpidius at Haran on p. 37; of S. Thecla at Seleucia in Isauria on p. 42; of S. Euphemia at Chalcedon on p. 43, and of S. John at Ephesus on p. 44. Among the other churches and holy sites Etheria visited (besides those in the Sinai district) mention may be made of the Church of Melchizedek (p. 28), the garden of S. John Baptist at Aenon (p. 27), and the grave of Job at Carneas (p. 29). She gives a full description on p. 20 of the scheme of devotions she and her companions used on each occasion, the order followed being this: prayer, reading, psalm, prayer; for less full accounts see pp. 7 f., 21 f., 26 f., 32, 35 f., 40 and 43.

14. *Officers of the Church.* Except Marthana, the deaconess (p. 42), who had been at Jerusalem and was afterwards in charge of nuns at Seleucia, the only one who needs to be specified here is the archdeacon. He is four times mentioned at Jerusalem as "lifting his voice" to announce the place of the next service and to invite the congregation to attend (pp. 63, 65, 70 and 87). The same official is mentioned as assisting the bishop when he confers minor orders in the *Statuta ecclesiae antiqua.* These used

INTRODUCTION xlv

to be considered as emanating from the fourth Council of Carthage (398), but they are now usually assigned to the end of the fifth century and held to be of Gallican origin (Duchesne *op. cit.* p. 132). In any case this is probably the earliest reference to the archdeacon in the East. He takes a prominent part in the services of the Coptic and Syrian Churches and is ordained to his office with special rites (see Denzinger, *Ritus Orientalium*, ii, pp. 10, 70, 86, and 142).

15. *Eulogiae.* At various places Etheria was presented with these after service, *e.g.* at Sinai, p. 5, where she explains them to be "gifts of the fruits grown on the mountain," and at Nebo on p. 21, and out of the garden or orchard of S. John the Baptist on p. 28. See explanation in footnotes *in loco* of this, which can hardly be considered a liturgical matter in the form in which Etheria mentions it.

11. THE CHURCHES IN JERUSALEM AND THE NEIGHBOURHOOD

In the Holy City itself Etheria mentions or refers to these Church buildings:—

1. The old Cathedral Church on Mount Sion, which in her day was no longer regularly used for service. The congregation, however, went there (her expression is *proceditur* or *itur*) on Wednesdays and Fridays in Lent, on Easter Day and its Octave, and on Whitsunday.

2. The *Anastasis* (Resurrection), on the traditional site of the Holy Sepulchre.

3. The *Sanctuary of the Cross*, on the traditional site of Golgotha (where the wood of the true Cross,

etc., were kept). This consisted of two parts: (a) *ante Crucem*, an open court (*atrium, locus subdivanus*) with cloisters, and (b) *post Crucem*, a smaller roofed-in building.

4. The *Martyrium* (*ecclesia maior*), which was also *post Crucem*, but exactly where in relation to 3 (b) is not quite clear (see conjectural plan on p. 137 of Bernard's edition); the great doors (*valvae maiores*) of it opened on to the market-place (*de quintana parte*).[1]

These last three buildings were set up by the Emperor Constantine in 337, the same year in which the Church of the Apostles (mentioned by Etheria, p. 44) had been completed by him in Constantinople. He also built the baptistery near the Anastasis referred to on p. 79.

The bishop's house (p. 50) was probably close by this group of buildings, no longer on Mount Sion.

The (eight-day) Dedication festival of the Anastasis and the Martyrium was held in September, in close connexion with the Discovery of the Cross and its Exaltation at the same time of the year and on the analogy of the Dedication of Solomon's Temple at the (autumn) Feast of Tabernacles.[2] A very large concourse assembled in Jerusalem on this occasion, not only of monks from Mesopotamia, Syria, and Egypt (especially the Thebaid), but also of bishops and clergy and the faithful laity, and the churches were decked out as at Easter and Epiphany (see pp. 95 f.).

---

[1] Eusebius (*Vit. Const.* iii. 39) gives a similar description of them.
[2] See Eus. *Vit. Const.* iv. 60, and Sozom. *H.E.* ii. 26.

INTRODUCTION

In the environs of Jerusalem she mentions:—

1. The Church at Bethlehem built and adorned by Constantine, with the help of his mother Helena[1] (p. 54). This was the appointed place for the night of the Epiphany and for the Ascension festival.

2. The Church *Eleona* (ἐλαιών) on the Mount of Olives, where was the cave in which our Lord used to teach His disciples.

3. The *Imbomon* (ἐν βωμῷ),[2] the traditional site of the Ascension, which was higher up on the Mount. It seems to have been rather an enclosed site with seats than a regular church (see p. 66).

4. The "graceful" Church in Gethsemane, which was no doubt lower down than Eleona (p. 71).

5. The Church on the road to Bethany where Mary, Lazarus's sister, met our Lord (p. 63).

6. The *Lazarium* in Bethany itself.

No particulars are to hand of these buildings that the present writer is aware of.

12. THE PRINCIPAL GREEK WORDS AND PHRASES USED

apotactites, see pp. xxix f. of Introduction.
archioteba (ἀρχέτυπος) = likeness (*i.e.* statue), p. 33.
ascetis, see p. xxix of Introduction.
campsemus (? κάμψωμεν) = turn, *i.e.* "go out of the way," p. 20.

---

[1] See Eus. *Vit. Const.* iii. 43.
[2] Βωμός here seems to represent the Heb. *bamah* = "high place" rather than to retain its usual sense of "altar," but, of course, with a Christian not a heathen association. *Bamah* is translated by βωμός in LXX, Jer. vii. 31, 32 (the altar of Tophet in the valley of Benhimmon), and in several other places in the prophets.

cata (κατά), five times as a prepn. with accus. = according to.
come (κώμη) = village, p. 15.
cepos tu agiu Johannu (κῆπος τοῦ ἁγίου Ἰωάννου), p. 27.
dendros alethias (δένδρον ἀληθείας), p. 16.
Eleona (= ἐλαιών), see p. xlvii of Introduction.
eortae (ἑορταί), see p. xxxviii of Introduction.
encenia (ἐγκαίνια) = dedication, p. 95.
eulogiae = blessings, see p. 5 *n*.
Imbomon (= ἐν βωμῷ), see p. xlvii of Introduction.
Kyrie eleison (κύριε ἐλέησον), see p. xliii of Introduction.
licinicon (λυχνικόν), p. 47.
monazontes (μονάζοντες) = *monachi* (μοναχοί), p. 45.
olosericus (ὁλοσηρικός) = all of silk, p. 53.
opu (? = ὄρος or ὅπου), *Melchizedek*, p. 28.
parthenae (παρθένοι) = *virgines*, p. 45.
petrinus (πετρινός) = rocky, p. 5.
siriste (συριστί) = in the Syriac language, p. 94.
thimiateria (θυμιατήρια) = censers, p. 49).

THE PILGRIMAGE OF ETHERIA

(*Much is wanting.*)

THE APPROACH TO SINAI

. . . .
were pointed out according to the Scriptures. In the meanwhile we came on foot to a certain place where the mountains, through which we were journeying, opened out and formed an infinitely great valley, quite flat and extraordinarily beautiful, and across the valley appeared Sinai, the holy mountain of God. And this place, where the mountains opened out, lies next to the place where are the graves of lust.[1] Now on reaching that spot, the holy guides who were with us told us, saying: "The custom is that prayer should be made by those who arrive here, when from this place the mount of God is first seen." And this we did. The whole distance from that place to the mount of God was about four miles across the aforesaid great valley.

For that valley is indeed very great, lying under the slope of the mount of God, and measuring, as far as we could judge by our sight, or as they told us, about sixteen miles in length, but they called its

[1] Eng. Bible, *Kibroth-hattaavah*, Num. xi. 34.

breadth four miles. We had, therefore, to cross that valley in order to reach the mountain. Now this is the great and flat valley wherein the children of Israel waited during those days when holy Moses went up into the mount of the Lord and remained there forty days and forty nights.[1] This moreover is the valley in which the calf was made,[2] and the spot is shown to this day, for a great stone stands fixed there on the very site. This also is the same valley at the head of which is the place where, while holy Moses was feeding his father-in-law's flocks, God spake to him twice out of the burning bush.[3] And as our route was first to ascend the mount of God, which is in sight here—[because] the ascent was easier by the way we were coming—and then to descend to the head of the valley where the bush was, that being the easier descent, so we determined, having first seen all that we desired, to descend from the mount of God so as to arrive at the place of the bush, and thence to return on our journey throughout the whole length of the valley, together with the men of God, who there showed us each place which is mentioned in the Scriptures. And so it was done. Thus, going from that spot where we had prayed when we arrived from Faran,[4] our route was to cross the middle of the head of that valley, and so turn to the mount of God.

Now the whole mountain group looks as if it were a single peak, but, as you enter the group, [you see that] there are more than one; the whole group however is called the mount of God. But that special peak which is crowned by the place where, as it is

[1] Exod. xxiv. 18. [2] Exod. xxxii.
[3] Exod. iii. 1 ff. [4] LXX, Φαράν : Eng. Bible, *Paran.*

written, the Glory of God descended, is in the centre of them all.[1] And though all the peaks in the group attain such a height as I think I never saw before, yet the central one, on which the Glory of God came down, is so much higher than them all, that when we had ascended it, all those mountains which we had thought to be high, were so much beneath us as if they were quite little hills. This is certainly very wonderful, and not, I think, without the favour of God, that while the central height, which is specially called Sinai, on which the Glory of the Lord descended, is higher than all the rest, yet it cannot be seen until you reach its very foot, though before you go up it. But after that you have fulfilled your desire and descend, you can see it from the other side, which you cannot do before you begin to ascend. This I had learned from information given by the brethren before we had arrived at the mount of God, and after I arrived I saw that it was manifestly so.

The Ascent of Sinai

We reached the mountain late on the sabbath, and arriving at a certain monastery, the monks who dwelt there received us very kindly, showing us every kindness; there is also a church and a priest there. We stayed there that night, and early on the Lord's Day, together with the priest and the monks who dwelt there, we began the ascent of the mountains one by one. These mountains are ascended with infinite toil, for you cannot go up gently by a spiral

[1] Exod. xix. 18, 20.

track, as we say snail-shell wise, but you climb straight up the whole way, as if up a wall, and you must come straight down each mountain until you reach the very foot of the middle one, which is specially called Sinai. By this way, then, at the bidding of Christ our God, and helped by the prayers of the holy men who accompanied us, we arrived, at the fourth hour, at the summit of Sinai, the holy mountain of God, where the law was given, that is, at the place where the Glory of the Lord descended on the day when the mountain smoked.[1] Thus the toil was great, for I had to go up on foot, the ascent being impossible in the saddle, and yet I did not feel the toil, on the side of the ascent, I say, I did not feel the toil, because I realized that the desire which I had was being fulfilled at God's bidding. In that place there is now a church, not great in size, for the place itself, that is the summit of the mountain, is not very great; nevertheless, the church itself is great in grace. When, therefore, at God's bidding, we had arrived at the summit, and had reached the door of the church, lo, the priest who was appointed to the church came from his cell and met us, a hale old man, a monk from early life, and an ascetic, as they say here, in short one worthy to be in that place; the other priests also met us, together with all the monks who dwelt on the mountain, that is, such as were not hindered by age or infirmity. No one, however, dwells on the very summit of the central mountain; there is nothing there excepting only the church and the cave where holy Moses was.[2] When the whole

---

[1] Exod. xix. 18. [2] Exod. xxxiii. 22.

passage from the book of Moses had been read in that place, and when the oblation had been duly made, at which we communicated, and as we were coming out of the church, the priests of the place gave us *eulogiae*,[1] that is, of fruits which grow on the mountain. For although the holy mountain Sinai is rocky throughout, so that it has not even a shrub on it, yet down below, near the foot of the mountains, around either the central height or those which encircle it, there is a little plot of ground where the holy monks diligently plant little trees and orchards, and set up oratories with cells near to them, so that they may gather fruits which they have evidently cultivated with their own hands from the soil of the very mountain itself. So, after we had communicated, and the holy men had given us *eulogiae*, and we had come out of the door of the church, I began to ask them to show us the several sites. Thereupon the holy men immediately deigned to show us the various places. They showed us the cave where holy Moses was when he had gone up again into the mount of God,[2] that he might receive the second tables after he had broken the former ones when the people sinned; they also deigned to show us the other sites which we desired to see, and those which they themselves well knew. But I would have you to know, ladies, reverend sisters, that from

---

[1] This word is still used in the Eastern Church for food which has been blessed by a priest, *e. g.* the first fruits from an orchard or a vineyard, viands on a table after "grace" has been pronounced over them, etc. Cf. Gen. xxxiii. 11, etc. See Brightman, *East. Lit.* p. 597, and for other more strictly liturgical uses, *ibid.* p. 577.

[2] Exod. xxxiv. 4.

the place where we were standing, round outside the walls of the church, that is from the summit of the central mountain, those mountains, which we could scarcely climb at first, seemed to be so much below us when compared with the central one on which we were standing, that they appeared to be little hills, although they were so very great that I thought that I had never seen higher, except that this central one excelled them by far.

From thence we saw Egypt and Palestine, and the Red Sea and the Parthenian Sea,[1] which leads to Alexandria and the boundless territories of the Saracens, all so much below us as to be scarcely credible, but the holy men pointed out each one of them to us.

HOREB

Having then fulfilled all the desire with which we had hastened to ascend, we began our descent from the summit of the mount of God which we had ascended to another mountain joined to it, which is called Horeb, where there is a church. This is that Horeb where was holy Elijah the prophet, when he fled from the face of Ahab the king, and where God spake to him and said: *What doest thou here, Elijah ?*[2] as it is written in the books of the Kings. The cave where holy Elijah lay hid is shown to this day before the door of the church which is there. A stone altar also is shown which holy Elijah raised to make an offering to God ; thus the holy men deigned to show

[1] *i.e.* the eastern end of the Mediterranean : see Introduction, p. xviii. *n.*
[2] 1 Kings xix. 9.

us each place. There, too, we made the oblation, with very earnest prayer, and also read the passage from the book of the Kings; for it was our special custom that, when we had arrived at those places which I had desired to visit, the appropriate passage from the book should always be read. The oblation having been made there, we came to another place not far off, which the priests and monks pointed out to us, where holy Aaron had stood with the seventy elders, when holy Moses was receiving the law from the Lord for the children of Israel.[1] In that place, although it is not covered in, there is a great rock which has a flat surface, rounded in shape, on which those holy men are said to have stood; there is also in the midst of it a kind of altar made of stones. The passage from the book of Moses was read there, and one psalm, suitable to the place. Then, after prayer had been made, we descended thence.

The Bush

And now it began to be about the eighth hour, and there were still three miles left before we could get out of the mountains which we had entered late on the previous day; we had not, however, to go out on the same side by which we had entered, as I said above, because it was necessary that we should walk past and see all the holy places and the cells that were there, and thus come out at the head of the valley, as I said above, that is of the valley that lies under the mount of God. It was necessary for us to come out

[1] Exod. xxiv. 9-14.

at the head of the valley, because there were very many cells of holy men there, and a church in the place where the bush is, which same bush is alive to this day and throws out shoots. So having made the whole descent of the mount of God we arrived at the bush about the tenth hour. This is that bush which I mentioned above, out of which the Lord spake in the fire to Moses, and the same is situated at that spot at the head of the valley where there are many cells and a church. There is a very pleasant garden in front of the church, containing excellent and abundant water, and the bush itself is in this garden. The spot is also shown hard by where holy Moses stood when God said to him: *Loose the latchet of thy shoe*, and the rest.[1] Now it was about the tenth hour when we had arrived at the place, and so, as it was late, we could not make the oblation, but prayer was made in the church and also at the bush in the garden, and the passage from the book of Moses was read according to custom. Then, as it was late, we took a meal with the holy men at a place in the garden before the bush; we stayed there also, and next day, rising very early, we asked the priests that the oblation should be made there, which was done.

The Sites in the Valley and the Return to Faran

And as our route lay through the middle and along the length of the valley—the same valley, as I said above, where the children of Israel sojourned while

[1] Exod. iii. 5.

Moses ascended into the mount of God and descended thence—so the holy men showed us each place that we came to in the whole valley. At the top of the head of the valley where we had stayed and had seen the bush out of which God spake in the fire to holy Moses, we had seen also the spot on which holy Moses had stood before the bush when God said to him: *Loose the latchet of thy shoe, for the place whereon thou standest is holy ground.*[1] In like manner they began to show us the other sites when we set out from the bush. They showed us the place where the camps of the children of Israel were in those days when Moses was in the mount. They also showed us the place where the calf was made, for a great stone is there to this day, fixed on the very spot. Then, too, as we were going on the other side we saw the top of the mountain which overlooks the whole valley; from which place holy Moses saw the children of Israel engaged in dancing at the time when they had made the calf.[2] They showed us a great rock in the place where holy Moses, as he was descending with Joshua the son of Nun, in his anger brake the tables that he was carrying, on the same rock. They showed us where they all had their dwelling places in the valley, the foundations of which dwelling places appear to this day, round in form and made with stone. They showed us also the place where holy Moses, when he returned from the mount, bade the children of Israel run *from gate to gate.*[3] They showed us also the place where the calf which Aaron had made for them was burnt at holy Moses' bidding. They showed

---
[1] Exod. iii. 5.   [2] Exod. xxxii. 19.
[3] Exod. xxxii. 27.

us also the stream of which holy Moses made the children of Israel drink, as it is written in Exodus.[1] They showed us also the place where the seventy men received of the spirit that was upon Moses.[2] They showed us also the place where the children of Israel lusted for meat. They showed us also the place which is called a Burning, because part of the camp was consumed what time holy Moses prayed, and the fire ceased.[3] They showed us also the place where it rained manna and quails upon them.[4] Thus were shown to us (the sites of) all the events which in the sacred books of Moses are recorded to have occurred there, viz., in the valley which, as I have said, lies under the mount of God, holy Sinai. Now it would be too much to write of all these things one by one, for so great a number could not be remembered, but when your affection[5] shall read the holy books of Moses it will more quickly recognize the things that were done in that place. Moreover this is the valley where the Passover was celebrated when one year had been fulfilled after that the children of Israel were come out of the land of Egypt.[6] For the children of Israel abode in that valley for some time, that is, while holy Moses ascended into and descended from the

---

[1] Exod. xvii. 5; or possibly the reference is to xxxii. 20.
[2] Num. xi. 25.   [3] Eng. Bible, *Taberah*, Num. xi. 2, 3.
[4] Exod. xvi. 13, 14.
[5] In addressing her sisters thus, Etheria is following the fashion of her own and subsequent centuries. In the Coptic ostraca found in Egypt we have many parallel expressions; *e.g.* on an ostracon from Thebes we read: "I, Andreas, priest, salute the sweetness of thy honoured brotherhood" (Hall's *Coptic and Greek Texts*, p. 71), and again one monk writes to another: "My insignificance salutes thy brotherhood," *ibid.* p. 34.
[6] Num. ix. 5.

mount of God the first and the second time; they tarried there also while the tabernacle was being made, together with all things that were shown (to Moses) in the mount of God. The place also was shown to us where the tabernacle was set up by Moses[1] for the first time, and all things were finished which God had bidden Moses in the mount that they should be made. At the very end of the valley we saw the graves of lust,[2] at the place where we resumed our route, that is where, leaving the great valley, we re-entered the way by which we had come, between the mountains of which I spoke above. On the same day we came up with the other very holy monks who, through age or infirmity, were unable to meet us in the mount of God for the making of the oblation, who yet deigned to receive us very kindly, when we reached their cells. So now that, together with the holy men who dwelt there, we had seen all the holy places we desired, as well as all the places which the children of Israel had touched in going to and from the mount of God, we returned to Faran in the name of God. And although I ought always to give thanks to God in all things, not to speak of these so great favours which He has deigned to confer on me, unworthy as I am, that I should journey through all these places, although I deserved it not, yet I cannot sufficiently thank even all those holy men who deigned with willing mind to receive my littleness in their cells and to guide me surely through all the places which I was always seeking, according to the holy Scriptures. Moreover, many of these holy men who dwelt on or around the

---

[1] Exod. xl. 17.   [2] Num. xi. 34.

mount of God deigned to escort us back to Faran, but these were of greater bodily strength.

Faran to Clysma

Now when we had arrived at Faran, which is thirty-five miles distant from the mount of God, we were obliged to stay there for two days to rest ourselves. On the third day, hastening thence, we came to a station in the desert of Faran, where we had stayed on our outward journey, as I said above. On the next day we came to water, and, travelling for a little while among the mountains, we arrived at a station which was on the sea, at the place where the route leaves the mountains, and begins to run continuously by the sea.[1] It runs by the sea in such a manner that at one time the waves touch the feet of the animals, while at another the course is through the desert, a hundred, two hundred, and sometimes even more than five hundred paces from the sea, for there is no sort of a road there, the whole being sandy desert. The inhabitants of Faran, who are accustomed to travel there with their camels, put signs in different places, and make for these signs when they travel in the day time, but the camels mark the signs at night. In short, the inhabitants of Faran travel more quickly and safely by night in that place, being accustomed thereto, than other men can travel in places where there is a clear road. Thus on our return journey we emerged from the mountains

[1] Professor Flinders Petrie in commenting on this passage, tells me: "The route along the west coast is very truly described, and is striking after being some days entirely in the desert."

at the place where we entered them on our journey out, and so turned towards the sea. So also did the children of Israel return from Sinai, the mount of God, to this place by the way they had come, that is, to the place where we left the mountains and reached the Red Sea. But while we turned back from this spot along the route by which we had made our journey out, the children of Israel marched hence on their own way, as it is written in the books of holy Moses.[1] So we returned to Clysma by the same route and the same stations by which we had come out, and when we had arrived at Clysma we were obliged to stay there also for rest, because we had travelled hard along the sandy way of the desert.

CLYSMA TO THE CITY OF ARABIA

Now although I had been acquainted with the land of Goshen ever since I was in Egypt for the first time, yet [I visited it again] in order that I might see all the places which the children of Israel touched on their journey out from Rameses, until they reached the Red Sea at the place which is now called Clysma from the fort which is there. I desired therefore that we should go from Clysma to the land of Goshen,[2] that is, to the city called Arabia, which city is in the land of Goshen. The whole territory is called after the city, the land of Arabia, the land of Goshen, although it is part of Egypt. It is much better land than all the rest of Egypt. From Clysma, that is from the

[1] Num. x. 12 and xxxiii. 36.
[2] *Gesse* in the text, *cf.* Gen. xlvi. 34, LXX, ἐν γῇ Γέσεμ 'Αραβίᾳ.

Red Sea, there are four desert stations, but though in the desert, yet there are military quarters at the stations with soldiers and officers who always escorted us from fort to fort. On that journey the holy men who were with us, clergy and monks, showed us all the places which I was always seeking in accordance with the Scriptures; some of these were on the left, some on the right of our path, some were far distant from, and some near to our route. For I hope that your affection will believe me [when I say that], as far as I could see, the children of Israel marched in such wise that as far as they went to the right, so far did they turn back to the left; as far as they went forward, so far did they return backward, journeying thus until they reached the Red Sea. Epauleum [1] was shown to us from the opposite side, when we were at Migdol,[2] where there is now a fort with an officer set over soldiers to maintain Roman discipline. These escorted us thence, according to custom, to another fort, and Baal-zephon [3] was shown to us, when we were at that place.[4] It is a plain above the Red Sea, along the side of the mountain which I mentioned above, where the children of Israel cried out when they saw the Egyptians coming after them. Etham [5] also was shown to us, which is on the edge of the wilderness, as it is written, also Succoth, which is a slight elevation in the middle of a valley, and by this

---

[1] *Epauleum.* ἀπέναντι τῆς ἐπαύλεως, Exod. xiv. 2, LXX, i.e. *opposite the military quarters.* The Eng. Bible has *before Pi-hahiroth.*
[2] *Magdalum* in text. Μαγδώλου, Exod. xiv. 2, LXX.
[3] *Belsefon* in text. Βεελσεπφών, Exod. xiv. 2, LXX.
[4] Exod. xiv. 10.
[5] *Oton* in text. Ὀθόμ, Exod. xiii. 20, LXX.

little hill the children of Israel encamped. This is the place where the law of the Passover was received.[1] The city of Pithom, which the children of Israel built,[2] was shown to us on the same journey at the place where, leaving the lands of the Saracens, we entered the territory of Egypt; the same Pithom is now a fort. The city of Hero,[3] which existed at the time when Joseph met his father Jacob as he came, as it is written in the book of Genesis, is now a *come*,[4] though a large one—a village as we say. This village has a church and martyr-memorials, and many cells of holy monks, so that we had to alight to see each of them, in accordance with the custom which we had. The village is now called Hero; it is situated at the sixteenth milestone from the land of Goshen, and it is within the boundaries of Egypt; moreover, it is a very pleasant spot, for an arm of the Nile flows there. Then, leaving Hero, we came to the city which is called Arabia, situated in the land of Goshen, for it is written concerning it that Pharaoh said to Joseph, *In the best of the land of Egypt make thy father and brethren to dwell, in the land of Goshen, in the land of Arabia.*[5]

RAMESES

Rameses is four miles from the city of Arabia, and in order to arrive at the station of Arabia, we passed through the midst of Rameses. The city of Rameses is now open country, without a single habitation, but

---

[1] Exod. xii. 43 ff. [2] Exod. i. 11.
[3] *Hero.* The LXX has (Gen. xlvi. 29) Ἡρώων πόλιν, the Eng. Bible, *Goshen.* For the "city of Arabia" (? Thou) see p. xix.
[4] Greek κώμη, *a village.* [5] Gen. xlvii. 6.

it is certainly traceable, since it was great in circumference and contained many buildings, for its ruins appear to this day in great numbers, just as they fell. There is nothing there now except one great Theban stone, on which are carved two statues of great size, which they say are those of the holy men, Moses and Aaron, raised in their honour by the children of Israel. There is also a sycomore tree, which is said to have been planted by the patriarchs; it is certainly very old, and therefore very small, though it still bears fruit. And all who have any indisposition go there and pluck off twigs, and it benefits them. This we learned from information given by the holy bishop of Arabia, who himself told us the name of the tree in Greek—*dendros alethiæ,* or as we say, the tree of truth. This holy bishop deigned to meet us at Rameses; he is an elderly man, truly pious from the time he became a monk, courteous, most kind in receiving pilgrims, and very learned in the Scriptures of God. He, after deigning to give himself the trouble of meeting us, showed us everything there and told us about the aforesaid statues, as well as about the sycomore tree. This holy bishop also informed us how Pharaoh, when he saw that the children of Israel had escaped him, before he set out after them, went with all his army into Rameses and burnt the whole city which was very great, and then set out thence in pursuit of the children of Israel.

Epiphany at the City of Arabia
Return to Jerusalem

Now it fell out by a very happy chance that the day on which we came to the station of Arabia was

RED GRANITE GROUP OF RAMESES II. AND THE GOD ATMU, FOUND AT RAAMSES, NOW TELL RETABEH. PROBABLY THE FIGURES LATER CALLED MOSES AND AARON.
(*From "Hyksos and Israelite Cities." Pl. XXXII.*)

[*Facing page* 16

the eve of the most blessed day of the Epiphany, and the vigils were to be kept in the church on the same day. Wherefore the holy bishop detained us there for some two days, a holy man and truly a man of God, well known to me from the time when I had been in the Thebaid. He became a holy bishop after being a monk, for he was brought up from a child in a cell, for which reason he is so learned in the Scriptures and chastened in his whole life, as I said above. From this place we sent back the soldiers who according to Roman discipline had given us the help of their escort as long as we had walked through suspected places. Now, however, as the public road —which passed by the city of Arabia and leads from the Thebaid to Pelusium—ran through Egypt, there was no need to trouble the soldiers further. Setting out thence we pursued our journey continuously through the land of Goshen, among vines that yield wine and vines that yield balsam, among orchards, highly cultivated fields and very pleasant gardens, our whole route lying along the bank of the river Nile among oft-recurring estates, which were once the homesteads of the children of Israel. And why should I say more? for I think that I have never seen a more beautiful country than the land of Goshen. And travelling thus for two days from the city of Arabia through the land of Goshen continuously, we arrived at Tatnis,[1] the city where holy Moses was born. This city of Tatnis was once Pharaoh's metropolis. Now

[1] *Tatnis*, i.e. *Zoan* (Numb. xiii. 22), but Archbp. Bernard conjectures *Taphnis*, in which case the place would be the *Tahpanhes* of Jer. xliii. 7 ff. (LXX Ταφνάς). For its connexion with "Pharaoh" see Hastings' *D.B.* vol. iv. p. 674. The birth-place of Moses is not mentioned in the Bible.

although I had already known these places—as I said above—when I had been at Alexandria and in the Thebaid, yet I wished to learn thoroughly all the places through which the children of Israel marched on their journey from Rameses to Sinai, the holy mountain of God; this made it necessary to return to the land of Goshen and thence to Tatnis. We set out from Tatnis and, walking along the route that was already known to me, I came to Pelusium. Thence I set out again, and journeying through all those stations in Egypt through which we had travelled before, I arrived at the boundary of Palestine. Thence in the Name of Christ our God I passed through several stations in Palestine and returned to Aelia,[1] that is Jerusalem.

Visit to the Jordan Valley

Having spent some time there, at God's bidding my will was to go as far as Arabia, to mount Nebo, where God commanded Moses to go up, saying to him: *Get thee up into the mountain Arabot,[2] into Mount Nebo, which is in the land of Moab, that is over against Jericho, and behold the land of Canaan, which I give unto the children of Israel for a possession, and die in the Mount whither thou goest up.* So Jesus our God, who will not forsake them that hope in Him, deigned to give effect to this my wish. Wherefore

---

[1] *Helia* in the text. Aelia Capitolina was the name given to the colony, which the Emperor Hadrian set up on Mount Sion A.D. 132. The retention of the name by an ecclesiastic like Etheria points to an early rather than a late date for her visit: see Heinichen on Eus., *H.E.* iv. 6.

[2] The LXX here (Deut. xxxii. 49 f.) has Ἀβαρείν (Eng. Bible, *Abarim*). The Pilgrim has apparently put *Arabot* (LXX Ἀραβώθ = plains in Heb.) by mistake. See note 4 on p. 19.

setting out from Jerusalem and journeying with holy men, with a priest and deacons from Jerusalem and with certain brothers, that is monks, we came to that spot on the Jordan where the children of Israel had crossed when holy Joshua, the son of Nun, had led them over Jordan, as it is written in the book of Joshua, the son of Nun.[1] The place where the children of Reuben and of Gad and the half tribe of Manasseh had made an altar was shown us a little higher up[2] on that side of the river-bank where Jericho is. Crossing the river we came to a city called Livias,[3] which is in the plain where the children of Israel encamped at that time, for the foundations of the camp of the children of Israel and of their dwellings where they abode appear there to this day. The plain is a very great one, lying under the mountains of Arabia above the Jordan; it is the place of which it is written:[4] *And the children of Israel wept for Moses in the Arabot Moab on the Jordan over against Jericho, forty days.* This is the place where, after Moses' death, Joshua the son of Nun was straightway *filled with the spirit of wisdom, for Moses had laid his hands upon him*, as it is written.[5] This is the place where Moses wrote the book of Deuteronomy, and where he *spake in the ears of all the congregation of Israel the*

---

[1] Josh. iii. 14; xxii. 10, 11.

[2] *i e.* on the west side.

[3] This is the *Beth-haran* of Numb. xxxii. 36 and Josh. xiii. 27, which was rebuilt and called Livias by Herod the Tetrarch in honour of the Empress Livia.

[4] Deut. xxxiv. 8. The LXX has: ἐν Ἀραβὼθ Μωάβ ἐπὶ τοῦ Ἰορδάνου κατὰ Ἱερειχὼ τριάκοντα ἡμέρας. The Eng. Bible puts "plains of Moab" instead of "Arabot M." The Pilgrim's "forty days" for "thirty" is no doubt an error.

[5] Deut. xxxiv. 9.

words of this song until it was ended; it is written in the book of Deuteronomy.[1] Here holy Moses, the man of God, blessed the children[2] of Israel one by one, in order, before his death.[3] So when we had arrived at this plain, we went to the very spot, and prayer was made; here, too, a certain part of Deuteronomy was read, as well as his song, with the blessings which he pronounced over the children of Israel; after the reading, prayer was made a second time, and giving thanks to God, we moved on thence. For it was always customary with us that, whenever we succeeded in reaching the places we desired to visit, prayer should first be made there, then the lection should be read from the book, then one appropriate psalm should be said, then prayer should be made again. At God's bidding we always kept to this custom, whenever we were able to come to the places we desired. After this, that the work begun should be accomplished, we began to hasten in order to reach mount Nebo. As we went, the priest of the place, *i.e.* Livias, whom we had prayed to accompany us from the station, because he knew the places well, advised us, saying: "If you wish to see the water which flows from the rock, which Moses gave to the children of Israel when they were thirsty, you can see it if you are willing to undertake the labour of going about six miles out of the way." When he had said this, we very eagerly wished to go, and turning at once out of our way, we followed the priest who led us. In that place there is a little church under a mountain, not Nebo, but

---

[1] Deut. xxxi. 30.   [2] *i.e.* the tribes.   [3] Deut. xxxiii.

THE PILGRIMAGE OF ETHERIA

another height behind, yet not far from Nebo. Many truly holy monks dwell there, whom they call here ascetics.

These holy monks deigned to receive us very kindly, and permitted us to go in to greet them. When we had entered and prayer had been made with them, they deigned to give us *eulogiae*,[1] which they are wont to give to those whom they receive kindly. There, in the midst, between the church and the cells, there flows from out of the rock a great stream of water, very beautiful and limpid, and excellent to the taste. Then we asked those holy monks who dwelt there what was this water of so good a flavour, and they said: "This is the water which holy Moses gave to the children of Israel in this desert."[2] So prayer was made there according to custom, the lection was read from the books of Moses and one psalm said, then—with the holy clergy and monks who had come with us—we went out to the mountain. Many of the holy monks also who dwelt by that water, and who could undertake the labour, deigned to ascend mount Nebo with us. So setting out thence, we arrived at the foot of mount Nebo, which was very high; nevertheless the greater part could be ascended sitting on asses, though a little bit was steeper and had to be climbed laboriously on foot, which was done.

[1] Archbp. Bernard translates this "gifts of blessing." Small loaves, called "blessings" were sent by ecclesiastics to one another. See *supra*, p. 5. Cf. Bigg, *Wayside Studies in Eccles. History*, p. 38.
[2] Cf. Num. xx. 11.

Mount Nebo

We arrived, then, at the summit of the mountain, where there is now a church of no great size, on the very top of mount Nebo. Inside the church, in the place where the pulpit is, I saw a place a little raised, containing about as much space as tombs usually contain. I asked the holy men what this was, and they answered: "Here was holy Moses laid by the angels, for, as it is written: *No man knoweth of his burial*,[1] since it is certain that he was buried by the angels. His tomb, indeed, where he was laid, is [not[2]] shown to this day; for as it was shown to us by our ancestors who dwelt here where [he was laid], so do we show it to you, and our ancestors said that this tradition was handed down to them by their own ancestors." So prayer was made anon, and all things that we were accustomed to do in their order in every place were done here also, and we began to go out of the church. Then they who knew the place—the priests and holy monks—said to us: "If you wish to see the places that are mentioned in the books of Moses, come out of the door of the church, and from the very summit, from the side on which they are visible from here, look and see,[3] and we will tell you each place that is visible from hence." Then we rejoiced greatly and immediately came out. From the door of the church

---

[1] Deut. xxxiv. 6. Archbp. Bernard translates *sepulturam*, *how he was buried*, and his note *in loc.* is: "I have followed Geyer in supposing that the monks interpreted *sepultura* of the *act* rather than of the *place* of burial: in no other way is it possible to make sense of the passage."

[2] Geyer, note *in loc.*, thinks that the *non* should be deleted.

[3] Cf. Lam. i. 12.

THE PILGRIMAGE OF ETHERIA 23

we saw the place where the Jordan runs into the Dead Sea, which place appeared below us as we stood. On the opposite side we saw not only Livias, which was on the near side of Jordan, but also Jericho, which was beyond Jordan; to so great a height rose the lofty place where we stood, before the door of the church. The greatest part of Palestine, the land of promise, was in sight, together with the whole land of Jordan, as far as it could be seen with our eyes. On the left side we saw all the lands of the Sodomites and Segor[1] which is the only one of the five cities that exists to-day. There is a memorial of it, but nothing appears of those other cities but a heap of ruins, just as they were turned into ashes. The place where was the inscription concerning Lot's wife was shown to us, which place is read of in the Scriptures.[2] But believe me, reverend ladies, the pillar itself cannot be seen, only the place is shown, the pillar is said to have been covered by the Dead Sea. Certainly when we saw the place we saw no pillar, I cannot therefore deceive you in this. The bishop of the place, that is of Segor, told us that it is now some years since the pillar could be seen. The spot where the pillar stood is about six miles from Segor, and the water now covers the whole of this space. Then we went to the right side of the church, out of doors and opposite to us two cities were pointed out, the one Esebon,[3] now called Exebon, which belonged to Seon, king of the Amorites, and the other, now called

[1] LXX Σήγωρ, Eng. Bible, Zoar. Gen. xiv. 2; Deut. xxxiv. 3.
[2] Gen. xix. 23-26. ? *titulus* (inscription) = στηλή (tombstone here.
[3] LXX 'Εσεβών, Eng. Bible, Heshbon. Numb. xxi, 26; Deut, iv. 46.

Sasdra,[1] the city of Og the king of Basan. Fogor,[2] which was a city of the kingdom of Edom, was also pointed out from thence, opposite to us. All these cities which we saw were situated on mountains, but a little below them the ground seemed to be flatter. Then we were told that in the days when holy Moses and the children of Israel had fought against those cities, they had encamped there, and indeed the signs of a camp were visible there. [From] the side of the mountain which I have called the left, which was over the Dead Sea, a very sharp-cut mountain was shown to us, which was formerly called Agri specula.[3] This is the mountain on which Balak the son of Beor placed Balaam the sooth-sayer to curse the children of Israel, and God refused to permit it, as it is written. Then, having seen everything that we desired, we returned in the Name of God through Jericho back to Jerusalem along the whole of the route by which we had come.

Visit to Ausitis

Now after some time I wished to go to the region of Ausitis[4] to visit the tomb of holy Job, for the sake of prayer. For I used to see many holy monks coming thence to Jerusalem to visit the holy places for the sake of prayer, who, giving information of everything concerning those places, increased my desire to

---

[1] LXX Ἐδράειμ, Eng. Bible, Edrei. Numb. xxi. 33; Deut. iii. 10.

[2] LXX Φογώρ, Eng. Bible, Peor. Numb. xxiii. 28; Deut. iv. 46.

[3] *i.e.* the ἀγροῦ σκοπιά (peak of the field) of the LXX. Numb. xxiii. 14. The Eng. Bible has "the field of Zophim."

[4] LXX Αὐσῖτις, Eng. Bible Uz, Job i. 1.

THE PILGRIMAGE OF ETHERIA 25

undertake the toil of going to them also, if indeed that can be called toil by which a man sees his desire to be fulfilled. So I set out from Jerusalem with the holy men who deigned to give me their company on my journey—they themselves also going for the sake of prayer—making my journey from Jerusalem through eight stations to Carneas. The city of Job is now called Carneas, but it was formerly called Dennaba,[1] in the land of Ausitis, on the confines of Idumea and Arabia. Travelling on this journey I saw on the bank of the river Jordan a very beautiful and pleasant valley abounding in vines and trees, for much excellent water was there, and in that valley there was a large village, which is now called Sedima. The village, which is situated in the middle of the level ground, has in its midst a little hill of no great size, shaped as large tombs are wont to be. There is a church on the summit and down below, around the little hill great and ancient foundations appear, while in the village itself some grave-mounds still remain. When I saw this pleasant place I asked what it was, and it was told me:[2] "This is the city of king Melchizedek, which was called Salem, but now, through the corruption of the language, the village is called Sedima. On the top of the little hill, which is situated in the midst of the village, the building that you see is a church, which is now called in the Greek language *opu Melchisedech*. For this is the

---

[1] Eng. Bible, Dinhabah, Gen. xxxvi. 32; 1 Chron. i. 43.
[2] See Gen. xiv. 8 and 18. The Pilgrim seems to identify Salem with Salim: see Hastings' *D.B.* under both names. Gamurrini conjectures that *opu* here and below stands for ὄρος = hill: but ? for ὅπου = where (Bernard). She never confuses ρ with ρ elsewhere.

place where Melchizedek offered pure sacrifices—that is bread and wine—to God, as it is written of him."

THE CITY OF MELCHIZEDEK

Directly I heard this, we alighted from our beasts, and lo! the holy priest of the place and the clergy deigned to meet us, and straightway receiving us led us up to the church. When we had arrived there, prayer was first said according to custom, then the passage from the book of holy Moses was read, then one psalm suitable to the place was said, then, after prayer made, we came down. When we had come down the holy priest addressed us. He was an elderly man, well taught in the Scriptures, and he had presided over the place from the time he had been a monk, to whose life many bishops—as we learned afterwards—bore great testimony, saying that he was worthy to preside over the place where holy Melchizedek—when Abraham was coming to meet him—was the first to offer pure sacrifices to God. When we had come down from the church, as I said above, the holy priest said to us: "Behold, these foundations which you see around the little hill are those of the palace of king Melchizedek. For from his time to the present day if any one wishes to build himself a house here, and so strikes on these foundations, he sometimes finds little fragments of silver and bronze. And this way which you see passing between the river Jordan and this village is the way by which holy Abraham returned to Sodom, after the slaughter of Chedorlaomer[1] king

---

[1] In Gen. xiv. 1 Chedorlaomer is called king of Elam and Tidal, king of Goiim (or nations, LXX ἐθνῶν).

of nations, and where holy Melchizedek, the king of Salem, met him."

ÆNON

Then, because I remembered that it was written [1] that S. John had baptized in Ænon near to Salim, I asked him how far off that place was. The holy priest answered: "It is near, two hundred paces off, and, if you wish, I will now lead you there on foot. This large and pure stream of water, which you see in this village, comes from that spring." Then I began to thank him and to ask him to lead us to the place, which was done. So we began to go with him on foot through the very pleasant valley, until we reached a most pleasant orchard, in the midst of which he showed us a spring of excellent and pure water, which sent out continuously a good stream. The spring had in front of it a sort of pool, where it appears that S. John the Baptist fulfilled his ministry. Then the holy priest said to us: "This garden is called nothing else to this day than [2] *cepos tu agiu iohannu* in the Greek language, or as you say in Latin, *hortus sancti Johannis*. Many brethren, holy monks, direct their steps hither from various places that they may wash there." So at the spring, as in every place, prayer was made, the proper lection was read and an appropriate psalm was said, and everything that it was customary for us to do whenever we came to the holy places, we did there also. The holy priest also told us that to this day, at Easter, all they who are to be baptized in the village, that is in the church

---

[1] S. John iii. 23.
[2] κῆπος τοῦ ἁγίου Ἰωάννου (the garden of Saint John).

which is called *opus Melchisedech*,[1] are always baptized in this spring, returning early to vespers with the clergy and monks, saying psalms and antiphons, so that they who have been baptized are led back early from the fountain to the church of holy Melchizedek. Then, receiving *eulogiae*[2] out of the orchard of S. John the Baptist from the priest, as well as from the holy monks who had cells in the same orchard, and always giving thanks to God, we set out on the way we were going.

THE CITY OF ELIJAH. THE BROOK CHERITH

Then going for a time through the valley of the Jordan on the bank of the river, because our route lay that way for a while, we suddenly saw the city of the holy prophet Elijah, that is Thesbe, whence he had the name of Elijah the Tishbite.[3] There, to this day, is the cave wherein the holy man sat; there too is the tomb of holy Getha,[4] whose name we read in the books of the Judges. There too we gave thanks to God according to custom and pursued our journey. And as we journeyed that way we saw a very pleasant valley opening towards us on the left; it was very large and discharged a very great torrent into the Jordan, and in that valley we saw the cell of one who is now a brother, that is a monk. Then I, as I am very inquisitive, began to ask what was this valley where the holy monk had now made himself a cell,

---

[1] See p. 25, note 2. [2] See note above, p. 5.
[3] LXX ὁ Θεσβείτης ἐκ Θεσβῶν τῆς Γαλαάδ, 1 Kings xvii. 1 ; the A.V. has "the inhabitants," the R.V. "the sojourners of Gilead."
[4] *i.e.* Jephthah, Judg. xii. 7 (Geyer) or perhaps Jether, Judg. viii. 20 (Bernard).

for I did not think it was without reason. Then the holy men who were journeying with us, and who knew the place, said, " This is the valley of Corra,[1] where holy Elijah the Tishbite dwelt in the time of king Ahab,[2] when there was a famine, and at the bidding of God the raven used to bring him food, and he drank water of the torrent. For this brook which you see running through this valley into Jordan, is Corra." Wherefore giving thanks to God Who deigned to show us everything that we desired, unworthy as we were, we began to make our journey as on other days. And as we journeyed day by day, on the left side, whence on the opposite side we saw parts of Phœnicia, there suddenly appeared a great and high mountain which extended in length . . . .

[*A leaf is torn out.*]

BURIAL-PLACE OF JOB. RETURN TO JERUSALEM

. . . which holy monk and ascetic, after so many years spent in the desert, found it necessary to move and to go down to the city of Carneas, in order to advise the bishop and clergy of that time, according as it had been revealed to him, that they should dig in that place which had been shown to him ; which was done. And they, digging in that place which had been shown to him, found a cave, which they followed for about a hundred paces, when suddenly, as they dug, a stone tomb came to light, and when they had uncovered it, they found carved on its lid (the name)

[1] LXX Χορράθ, Eng. Bible, Cherith. 1 Kings xvii. 3.
[2] 1 Kings xvii. 4, etc.

Job. To this Job the church which you see was then built in that place, in such a manner that the stone with the body should not be moved, but that it should be placed, where the body had been found, and that the body should lie under the altar. That church, which was built by some tribune, has been unfinished to this day. Next morning we asked the bishop to make the oblation, which he deigned to do, and the bishop blessing us, we set out. There too we communicated, and always giving thanks to God we returned to Jerusalem, journeying through each of the stations through which we had passed three years before.

JOURNEY INTO MESOPOTAMIA

Having spent some time there in the Name of God, when three full years had passed since I came to Jerusalem, and having seen all the holy places which I had visited for the sake of prayer, my mind was to return to my country. I wished, however, at God's bidding, to go to Mesopotamia in Syria, to visit the holy monks who were there in great number, and who were said to be of such holy life as could hardly be described, and also for the sake of prayer at the memorial of S. Thomas the Apostle, where his body is laid entire. This is at Edessa. For Jesus our God by a letter which He sent to Abgar the king by the hand of Ananias the courier, promised that He would send S. Thomas thither, after that He Himself had ascended into Heaven.[1] The letter is kept with great reverence at the city of Edessa, where the memorial

---

[1] See Eus., *Hist. Eccl.* i. 13.

is. Now your affection may believe me that there is no Christian who having arrived at the holy places that are at Jerusalem, does not go on thither for the sake of prayer; it is at the twenty-fifth station from Jerusalem. And since from Antioch it is nearer to Mesopotamia, it was very convenient for me at God's bidding that as I was returning to Constantinople, and my way lying through Antioch, I should go thence to Mesopotamia. This then, at God's bidding, I did.

Antioch to Mesopotamia. The Crossing of the Euphrates

Then, setting out from Antioch to Mesopotamia in the Name of Christ our God, I journeyed through certain stations and cities of the province of Cœle-Syria, which is Antioch, and entering the borders of the province of Augustofratensis,[1] I came to the city of Gerapolis[2] which is the metropolis of Augustofratensis. And as this city is very beautiful and rich and abounds in everything, it was necessary for me to make a halt there, for the borders of Mesopotamia were not far distant. Then starting from Ierapolis,[2] I came, in the Name of God, at the fifteenth milestone to the river Euphrates, of which it is very well written that it is *the great river Euphrates*[3]; it is huge and, as it were, terrible, for it flows down with a current like the river Rhone, only the Euphrates is still greater. And as we had to cross in ships, and in large ships only, I waited there until after midday, and then in the Name

---
[1] *i.e.* Augusta Euphratensis.
[2] *i.e.* Hierapolis.   [3] Gen. xv. 18.

of God I crossed the river Euphrates and entered the borders of Mesopotamia in Syria.

Edessa

Then, journeying through certain stations, I came to a city whose name we read recorded in the Scriptures—Batanis,[1] which city exists to-day: it has a church with a truly holy bishop, both monk and confessor, and certain martyr-memorials. The city has a teeming population, and the soldiery with their tribune are stationed there. Departing thence, we arrived at Edessa in the Name of Christ our God, and, on our arrival, we straightway repaired to the church and memorial of saint Thomas. There, according to custom, prayers were made and the other things that were customary in the holy places were done; we read also some things concerning saint Thomas himself. The church there is very great, very beautiful and of new construction, well worthy to be the house of God, and as there was much that I desired to see, it was necessary for me to make a three days' stay there. Thus I saw in that city many memorials, together with holy monks, some dwelling at the memorials, while others had their cells in more secluded spots farther from the city. Moreover, the holy bishop of the city, a truly devout man, both monk and confessor, received me willingly and said: "As I see, daughter, that for the sake of devotion you have undertaken so great a labour in coming to these places from far-distant lands, if you are willing, we

[1] Bathnæ in Osrhoene (Bernard). There seems to be no reference to this place in Holy Scripture.

will show you all the places that are pleasant to the sight of Christians." Then, first thanking God, I besought the bishop much that he would deign to do as he said. He thereupon led me first to the palace of King Abgar, where he showed me a great marble statue of him—very much like him, as they said—having a sheen as if made of pearl. From the face of Abgar it seemed that he was a very wise and honourable man. Then the holy bishop said to me: "Behold King Abgar, who before he saw the Lord believed in Him that He was in truth the Son of God." There was another statue near, made of the same marble, which he said was that of his son Magnus; this also had something gracious in the face. Then we entered the inner part of the palace, and there were fountains full of fish such as I never saw before, of so great size, so bright and of so good a flavour were they. The city has no water at all other than that which comes out of the palace, which is like a great silver river.

The Story of King Abgarus

Then the holy bishop told me about the water, saying: "At some time, after that King Abgar had written to the Lord, and the Lord had answered King Abgar by Ananias the courier—as it is written in the letter itself—when some time had passed, the Persians came against the city and surrounded it. And straightway Abgar, bearing the letter of the Lord to the gate, with all his army, prayed publicly. And he said: "O Lord Jesus, Thou hadst promised us that none of our enemies should enter this city, and lo! the

Persians now attack us." And when the king had said this, holding the open letter in his uplifted hands, suddenly there came a great darkness outside the city before the eyes of the Persians, as they were approaching the city at a distance of about three miles, and they were so baffled by the darkness that they could hardly form their camp and surround the whole city about three miles off. So baffled were the Persians that they could never afterwards see the way to enter the city, but they surrounded it and shut it in with their hostile forces, at a distance of about three miles, for several months. Then, when they saw that they could by no means enter, they wished to slay those within the city by thirst. Now that little hill which you see, my daughter, over against the city, supplied it with water at that time, and the Persians, perceiving this, diverted the water from the city and made it to run near that place where they had made their camp. And on that day and at that hour when the Persians diverted the water, the fountains which you see in this place burst forth at once at God's bidding, and by the favour of God they remain here from that day to this. But the water which the Persians had diverted was dried up at that hour, so that they who were besieging the city had nothing to drink for even one day; which thing is plain to the present time, for no moisture of any sort has ever been seen there from that day to this. So, at God's bidding, Who had promised that this should come to pass, they were obliged to return to their own home in Persia. Moreover afterwards, as often as enemies determined to come and take the city, this letter was brought out and read in the gate, and straightway all

enemies were driven back by the will of God. The
holy Bishop also told me that the place where these
fountains broke forth had previously been open ground
within the city, lying under the palace of King Abgar,
which same palace had been situated on somewhat
higher ground, as was plainly visible. For the custom
was at that time that, whenever palaces were built,
they should always stand on higher ground. But after
that these fountains had burst forth here, then Abgar
built this palace for his son Magnus, whose statue I
saw near that of his father, so that the fountains
should be included in the palace. And when the
holy bishop had told me all these things, he said to
me: " Let us now go to the gate by which Ananias
the courier entered with the letter of which I spoke."
So when we had come to the gate, the bishop, standing, made a prayer and read us the letters ; then, after
he had blessed us, another prayer was made. Moreover the holy man told us that from the day on which
Ananias the courier entered it with the letter of the
Lord, the gate is kept to this day, that no one who is
unclean, nor any mourner, should pass through nor
should any dead body be borne out through it. The
holy bishop also showed us the memorial of Abgar
and of his whole family, very beautiful, but made in
the ancient style. He took us also to the palace
which King Abgar had at first, on the higher ground,
and if there were any other places he showed them to
us. It was very pleasant to me to receive from the holy
man himself the letters of Abgar to the Lord and of
the Lord to Abgar, which the holy bishop had read
to us there. For although I have copies at home, yet
it seemed to me more pleasant to receive them from

him, lest perhaps something less might have reached us at home, and indeed that which I received here is fuller. So if Jesus our God bids it, and I come home, you too shall read them, ladies, my own souls.

CHARRÆ (HARAN)

Then, after three days spent there, it was necessary for me to go still farther, to Charræ, as it is now called. In holy Scripture it is called Charran,[1] where holy Abraham dwelt, as it is written in Genesis when the Lord said unto Abram: *Get thee out of thy country, and from thy father's house, and go to Charran* and the rest.[2] And when I arrived at Charræ I went straightway to the church which is within the city, and soon I saw the bishop of the place, a truly holy man of God, both monk and confessor, who deigned to show us all the places there that we desired. He took us at once to the church, which is without the city on the spot where stood the house of holy Abraham; it stands on the same foundations, and it is made of the same stone, as the holy bishop said. When we had come to the church, prayer was made, the passage from Genesis was read, one psalm was said, and after a second prayer the bishop blessed us and we came out. Then he deigned to take us to the well whence holy Rebecca used to fetch water,[3] and the holy bishop said to us: "Behold the well whence holy Rebecca watered the camels of holy Abraham's servant Eleazar"; thus he deigned to show us each thing. Now at the church, which is outside the city,

[1] LXX Χαρράν, Eng. Bible Haran. Gen. xii. 4.
[2] Gen. xii. 1.   [3] Gen. xxiv. 15, etc.

as I said, ladies, reverend sisters, where Abraham's house was originally, there is now the martyr-memorial of a certain holy monk named Helpidius. It happened very pleasantly for us that we arrived on the day before the martyr's feast of saint Helpidius, which is on the twenty-third of April.[1] On that day it was of obligation that all the monks from all parts and from all the borders of Mesopotamia should come down to Charræ, even the greater ones who dwelt in solitude, whom they call ascetics. For this day is observed with great dignity there on account of the memorial of holy Abraham, whose house stood where the church now is, in which the body of the holy martyr is laid. So it happened to us very pleasantly beyond our expectations that we should see these holy monks of Mesopotamia, truly men of God, as well as those whose good report and manner of life had reached men's ears far and wide, whom I thought that I could not by any means see, not because it was impossible for God to give me this, Who had deigned to give me all things, but because I had heard that they never come down from their dwellings except on Easter Day and on this day. For they are men who do many wonders, and, moreover, I did not know in what month was the day of the martyr's feast which I have mentioned; but at God's bidding it came about that I arrived on the day that I had not hoped for. We stayed there two days, for the memorial day and for the sake of seeing those holy men, who

[1] The ancient Syriac Martyrology (A.D. 411/2), as printed by Lietzmann (*Drei Ält. Mart.* p. 12), gives Helpidios and Hermogenes the martyrs in Melitene (Cappadocia) on May 3rd, not April 23rd.

deigned to receive me very willingly for the sake of salutation, and to speak with me, of which I was not worthy. Nor were they seen there after the memorial day, for they sought the desert without delay in the night, each one returning to his own cell. In that city I found scarcely a single Christian excepting a few clergy and holy monks—if any such dwell in the city; all are heathen. And in like manner, as we gazed with great reverence at the place where the house of holy Abraham was at first for the sake of his memorial, so do those heathen gaze with great reverence at a place about a mile from the city, where are the memorials of Nahor and Bethuel. And since the bishop of that city is very learned in the Scriptures, I asked him, saying : " I beg of you, my lord, to tell me that which I desire to hear." And he said : " Tell me, daughter, what you wish, and I will tell it you, if I know it." Then I said : " I know by the Scriptures [1] that holy Abraham came to this place with his father Terah and with Sarah his wife, and with Lot his brother's son, but I have not read when Nahor and Bethuel came here ; I know only that afterwards Abraham's servant came to Charræ that he might seek Rebecca, the daughter of Bethuel, the son of Nahor, for Isaac the son of his master Abraham." [2] Then the holy bishop said to me : " Truly, daughter, it is written as you say, in Genesis, that holy Abraham came here with his relatives, but canonical Scripture does not say when Nahor and his relatives and Bethuel came here, but it is plain that they did come here afterwards, since their memorials are here at about a mile from the city. The Scripture does indeed

[1] Gen. xi. 31.   [2] Gen. xxiv. 10, 15.

relate [1] how holy Abraham's servant came here to take holy Rebecca, and how holy Jacob came here when he took to himself the daughters of Laban the Syrian." Then I asked where was the well where holy Jacob watered the flocks which Rachel, the daughter of Laban the Syrian, was feeding. The bishop said to me: "The place is six miles hence, near the village which then was the farm of Laban the Syrian, and if you wish to go there, we will go with you and show it to you; there are also many very holy monks and ascetics, and a holy church." I also asked the holy bishop where was that place of the Chaldees where Terah lived at first with his family,[2] and the holy bishop said to me: "The place, daughter, of which you ask, is at the tenth station hence, as you go into Persia. There are five stations from here to Nisibis, and five stations thence to Hur,[3] which was a city of the Chaldees, but there is now no access for Romans, for the Persians hold the whole country.[4] This district is specially called the Eastern; it is on the borders of the Romans, the Persians and the Chaldees." And many other things he deigned to tell me, as did also the other holy bishops and holy monks, but all they told us was from the Scriptures of God or of the acts of holy men, that is of monks, either the wonderful things that those already departed had done, or what those who are still in the body do daily, at any rate those who are ascetics. For I would not that your affection should think that the monks ever told me

---

[1] Gen. xxix. 1, 2, 4.   [2] Gen. xi. 28.
[3] Ur of the Chaldees. Gen. xi. 28.
[4] The Emperor Jovian had been forced to sign a treaty and surrender Nisibis and the district to Sapor in A.D. 363.

any other stories except from the Scriptures of God or else those of the acts of the greater monks.

RACHEL'S WELL. THE RETURN TO ANTIOCH

Now after two days which I spent there, the bishop took us to the well where holy Jacob had watered holy Rachel's flocks;[1] the well is six miles from Charræ, and in its honour a very great and beautiful holy church has been built hard by. When we had come to the well, prayer was made by the bishop, the passage from Genesis was read, one psalm suitable to the place was said and, after a second prayer, the bishop blessed us. We saw also, lying on a spot near the well, that very great stone which holy Jacob had moved away from the well, and which is shown to-day. No one dwells there around the well, except the clergy of the church which is there and the monks who have their cells near at hand, whose truly unheard-of mode of life the bishop described to us. Then, after prayer had been made in the church, I visited, in company with the bishop, the holy monks in their cells, giving thanks both to God and to them, who deigned with willing mind to receive me in their cells wherever I entered, and to address me in such words as were fitting to proceed out of their mouth. They deigned also to give me and all who were with me *eulogiae*,[2] such as is the custom for monks to give those whom they receive with willing mind into their cells.

[1] Gen. xxix. 10.
[2] See note above, p. 5.

THE PILGRIMAGE OF ETHERIA 41

And the place being in a large plain, a great village over against us was pointed out to me by the holy bishop, about five hundred paces from the well, through which village our route lay. This village, as the bishop said, was once the farm of Laban the Syrian, and is called Fadana;[1] in the village the memorial of Laban the Syrian, Jacob's father-in-law, was shown to me; the place was also shown to me where Rachel stole her father's images.[2] So, having seen everything in the Name of God, and bidding farewell to the holy bishop and the holy monks who had deigned to conduct us to the place, we returned by the route and by the stations through which we had come from Antioch.

ANTIOCH TO TARSUS

When I had got back to Antioch, I stayed there for a week, while the things that were necessary for our journey were being prepared. Then, starting from Antioch and journeying through several stations, I came to the province called Cilicia, which has Tarsus for its metropolis. I had already been at Tarsus on my way to Jerusalem, but as the memorial of saint Thecla is at the third station from Tarsus, in Hisauria, it was very pleasant for me to go there, especially as it was so very near at hand.

---

[1] *i.e.*, Paddan-Aram = plain of Aram (Syria), LXX Μεσοποταμία Συρίας. Gen. xxviii. 2. See Hastings' *D.B.* i. p. 138, for this name of Mesopotamia.

[2] Gen. xxxi. 19.

Visit to S. Thecla's Church. Return to Constantinople

So, setting out from Tarsus, I came to a certain city on the sea, still in Cilicia, which is called Pompeiopolis. Thence I entered the borders of Hisauria and stayed in a city called Coricus, and on the third day I arrived at a city which is called Seleucia in Hisauria;[1] on my arrival I went to the bishop, a truly holy man, formerly a monk, and in that city I saw a very beautiful church. And as the distance thence to saint Thecla, which is situated outside the city on a low eminence, was about fifteen hundred paces, I chose rather to go there in order to make the stay that I intended. There is nothing at the holy church in that place except numberless cells of men and of women. I found there a very dear friend of mine, to whose manner of life all in the East bore testimony, a holy deaconess named Marthana, whom I had known at Jerusalem, whither she had come for the sake of prayer; she was ruling over the cells of *apotactitae*[2] and virgins. And when she had seen me, how can I describe the extent of her joy or of mine? But to return to the matter in hand: there are very many cells on the hill and in the midst of it a great wall which encloses the church containing the very beautiful memorial. The wall

---

[1] Thecla is honoured as "protomartyr" in the East as well as in the West on Sept. 23rd or 24th. Tradition calls her a disciple of St. Paul at Iconium, but places her grave (as here) at Seleucia in Isauria. Justinian built a church in her memory at Constantinople. The *Anc. Syr. Mart.* does not mention her.

[2] See Introduction, pp. xxix f.

was built to guard the church because of the Hisauri, who are very malicious and who frequently commit acts of robbery, to prevent them from making an attempt on the monastery which is established there. When I had arrived in the Name of God, prayer was made at the memorial, and the whole of the acts of saint Thecla having been read, I gave endless thanks to Christ our God, who deigned to fulfil my desires in all things, unworthy and undeserving as I am. Then, after a stay of two days, when I had seen the holy monks and *apotactitae* who were there, both men and women, and when I had prayed and made my communion, I returned to Tarsus and to my journey. From Tarsus, after a halt of three days, I set out on my journey in the Name of God, and arriving on the same day at a station called Mansocrenae,[1] which is under Mount Taurus, I stayed there. On the next day, going under Mount Taurus, and travelling by the route that was already known to me, through each province that I had traversed on my way out, to wit, Cappadocia, Galatia, and Bithynia, I arrived at Chalcedon, where I stayed for the sake of the very famous martyr-memorial of saint Euphemia,[2] which was already known to me from a former time. On the next day, crossing the sea, I arrived at Constantinople, giving thanks to Christ our God who deigned to give me such grace, unworthy and undeserving as I am, for He had deigned to give me not only the will to go, but also the power of walking through the places

[1] *i.e.*, Mopsucrene (Bernard).
[2] Commemorated both East and West on Sept. 16th, but not given in *Anc. Syr. Mart.*

that I desired, and of returning at last to Constantinople. When I had arrived there, I went through all the churches—that of the Apostles and all the martyr-memorials, of which there are very many—and I ceased not to give thanks to Jesus our God, Who had thus deigned to bestow His mercy upon me. From which place, ladies, light of my eyes, while I send these (letters) to your affection, I have already purposed, in the Name of Christ our God, to go to Ephesus in Asia, for the sake of prayer, because of the memorial of the holy and blessed Apostle John. And if after this I am yet in the body, and am able to see any other places, I will either tell it to your affection in person, if God deigns to permit me this, or in anywise, if I have another project in mind, I will send you news of it in a letter. But do you, ladies, light of my eyes, deign to remember me, whether I am in the body or out of the body.

THE MOSAIC IN ST. PUDENZIANA AT ROME SAID TO BE IN PART OF THE FOURTH CENTURY

JERUSALEM

I

DAILY OFFICES

1. *Matins.*

NOW that your affection may know what is the order of service (*operatio*) day by day in the holy places, I must inform you, for I know that you would willingly have this knowledge. Every day before cockcrow all the doors of the Anastasis[1] are opened, and all the monks and virgins, as they call them here, go thither, and not they alone, but lay people also, both men and women, who desire to begin their vigil early. And from that hour to daybreak hymns are said[2] and psalms are sung responsively (*responduntur*), and antiphons in like manner; and prayer is made after each of the hymns. For priests, deacons, and monks in twos or threes take it in turn every day to say prayers after each of the hymns or antiphons. But when day breaks they begin to say the Matin hymns. Thereupon the bishop arrives with

---

[1] See Introduction, p. xlv.
[2] Etheria constantly uses *dicuntur, dicitur* applied to hymns and psalms—but she probably means "sung." See Introduction, pp. xxxix f.

the clergy, and immediately enters into the cave,[1] and from within the rails (*cancelli*) he first says a prayer for all, mentioning the names of those whom he wishes to commemorate; he then blesses the catechumens, afterwards he says a prayer and blesses the faithful. And when the bishop comes out from within the rails, every one approaches his hand,[2] and he blesses them one by one as he goes out, and the dismissal[3] takes place, by daylight.

2. *Sext and None.*

In like manner at the sixth hour all go again to the Anastasis, and psalms and antiphons are said, while the bishop is being summoned; then he comes

---

[1] See Introduction, pp. xlv f.

[2] The expression "to approach the bishop's hand" has given rise to much discussion. Archbp. Bernard and Professor Sayce both suggested it was for the purpose of kissing it. But an account given by Mrs. Gibson and Mrs. Lewis of their visit to the very ancient Coptic Monastery of Deyr Antonius on the Red Sea, seems to suggest another solution. They relate that when they attended Mass in the Church of the Monastery . . . "the Service lasted two hours, and towards its close all present, including ourselves, went up to the door of the sanctuary and received a blessing from the chief celebrant, which consisted mainly in his *laying a hand on our cheeks*." I submitted this as a possible explanation of Etheria's expression to Mgr. Duchesne and to Dom Cabrol and they both agreed it appeared to solve the difficulty. Dom Cabrol further suggested that this manner of conveying a blessing might be the origin of the *colaphus* or *soufflet* given in Confirmation in the Western Church. For further details of this Coptic Mass see *The Century Magazine*, Sept. 1904, article "Hidden Egypt," by Mrs. Lewis.

[3] It should be noted that the word *missa* in the text is almost always translated "dismissal," although it must on some occasions have meant "Mass." This, however, Etheria usually calls *oblatio* (*offerre*). For the ambiguity of the meaning attached to *missa*, see Introduction, pp. xl f.

as before, not taking his seat, but he enters at once within the rails in the Anastasis, that is in the cave, just as in the early morning, and as then, he again first says a prayer, then he blesses the faithful, and as he comes out from [within] the rails every one approaches his hand. And the same is done at the ninth hour as at the sixth.

3. *Vespers.*

Now at the tenth hour, which they call here *licinicon*,[1] or as we say *lucernare*, all the people assemble at the Anastasis in the same manner, and all the candles and tapers are lit, making a very great light. Now the light is not introduced from without, but it is brought forth from within the cave, that is from within the rails, where a lamp is always burning day and night, and the vesper psalms and antiphons are said, lasting for a considerable time. Then the bishop is summoned, and he comes and takes a raised seat, and likewise the priests sit in their proper places, and hymns and antiphons are said. And when all these have been recited according to custom, the bishop rises and stands before the rails, that is, before the cave, and one of the deacons makes the customary commemoration of individuals one by one. And as the deacon pronounces each name the many little boys who are always standing by, answer with countless voices: *Kyrie eleyson*, or as we say *Miserere Domine*.[2] And when the deacon has finished all that he has to say, first the bishop says a prayer and

---

[1] *i.e.* τὸ λυχνικόν.
[2] For this, see Introduction, p. xliii.

prays for all, then they all pray, both the faithful and catechumens together. Again the deacon raises his voice, bidding each catechumen to bow his head where he stands, and the bishop stands and says the blessing over the catechumens. Again prayer is made, and again the deacon raises his voice and bids the faithful, each where he stands, to bow the head, and the bishop likewise blesses the faithful. Thus the dismissal takes place at the Anastasis, and one by one all draw near to the bishop's hand. Afterwards the bishop is conducted from the Anastasis to the Cross [with] hymns, all the people accompanying him, and when he arrives he first says a prayer, then he blesses the catechumens, then another prayer is said and he blesses the faithful. Thereupon both the bishop and the whole multitude further proceed behind the Cross, where all that was done before the Cross is repeated, and they approach the hand of the bishop behind the Cross as they did at the Anastasis and before the Cross. Moreover, there are hanging everywhere a vast number of great glass chandeliers, and there are also a vast number of *cereofala*,[1] before the Anastasis, before the Cross and behind the Cross, for the whole does not end until darkness has set in. This is the order of daily services (*operatio*) at the Cross and at the Anastasis throughout the six days.

[1] *i.e.* candles on tall candlesticks (*Ducange*).

II

Sunday Offices

1. *Vigil.*

But on the seventh day,[1] that is on the Lord's Day, the whole multitude assembles before cockcrow, in as great numbers as the place can hold, as at Easter, in the basilica which is near the Anastasis, but outside the doors, where lights are hanging for the purpose. And for fear that they should not be there at cockcrow they come beforehand and sit down there. Hymns as well as antiphons are said, and prayers are made between the several hymns and antiphons, for at the vigils there are always both priests and deacons ready there for the assembling of the multitude, the custom being that the holy places are not opened before cockcrow. Now as soon as the first cock has crowed, the bishop arrives and enters the cave at the Anastasis; all the doors are opened and the whole multitude enters the Anastasis, where countless lights are already burning. And when the people have entered, one of the priests says a psalm to which all respond, and afterwards prayer is made; then one of the deacons says a psalm and prayer is again made, a third psalm is said by one of the clergy, prayer is made for the third time and there is a commemoration of all. After these three psalms and three prayers are ended, lo! censers are brought into the cave of the Anastasis so that the whole basilica

[1] Etheria here calls the Lord's Day the seventh day, but only because she has just before spoken of the six days that precede it.

of the Anastasis is filled with odours.[1] And then the bishop, standing within the rails, takes the book of the Gospel, and proceeding to the door, himself reads the (narrative of the) Resurrection of the Lord. And when the reading is begun, there is so great a moaning and groaning among all, with so many tears, that the hardest of heart might be moved to tears for that the Lord had borne such things for us. After the reading of the Gospel the bishop goes out, and is accompanied to the Cross by all the people with hymns, there again a psalm is said and prayer is made, after which he blesses the faithful and the dismissal takes place, and as he comes out all approach to his hand. And forthwith the bishop betakes himself to his house, and from that hour all the monks return to the Anastasis, where psalms and antiphons, with prayer after each psalm or antiphon, are said until daylight; the priests and deacons also keep watch in turn daily at the Anastasis with the people, but of the lay people, whether men or women, those who are so minded, remain in the place until daybreak, and those who are not, return to their houses and betake themselves to sleep.

2. *Morning Services.*

Now at daybreak because it is the Lord's Day, every one proceeds to the greater church, built by Constantine, which is situated in Golgotha behind the Cross, where all things are done which are customary

[1] Assuming the earlier date of this pilgrimage, we have probably here the earliest mention extant of incense being used in a Christian church at the time of public worship : see *Dictionary of Prayer Book*, p. 406, *s.v.*

everywhere[1] on the Lord's Day. But the custom here is that of all the priests who take their seats, as many as are willing, preach, and after them all the bishop preaches, and these sermons are always on the Lord's Day, in order that the people may always be instructed in the Scriptures and in the love of God. The delivery of these sermons greatly delays the dismissal from the church, so that the dismissal does [not] take place before the fourth or perhaps the fifth hour. But when the dismissal from the church is made in the manner that is customary everywhere, the monks accompany the bishop with hymns from the church to the Anastasis, and as he approaches with hymns all the doors of the basilica of the Anastasis are opened, and the people, that is the faithful, enter, but not the catechumens. And after the people the bishop enters, and goes at once within the rails of the cave of the martyrium. Thanks are first given to God, then prayer is made for all, after which the deacon bids all bow their heads, where they stand, and the bishop standing within the inner rails blesses them and goes out, each one drawing near to his hand as he makes his exit. Thus the dismissal is delayed until nearly the fifth or sixth hour. And in like manner it is done at *lucernare*, according to daily custom.

This then is the custom observed every day throughout the whole year except on solemn days, to the keeping of which we will refer later on. But among all things it is a special feature that they arrange that suitable psalms and antiphons are said on every occasion, both those said by night, or in the morning,

[1] This of course includes the celebration of the Eucharist.

as well as those throughout the day, at the sixth hour, the ninth hour, or at *lucernare*, all being so appropriate and so reasonable as to bear on the matter in hand. And they proceed to the greater church, which was built by Constantine, and which is situated in Golgotha, that is, behind the Cross, on every Lord's Day throughout the year except on the one Sunday of Pentecost, when they proceed to Sion, as you will find mentioned below; but even then they go to Sion before the third hour, the dismissal having been first made in the greater church.

* * * * * * *

[*A leaf is wanting.*]

III

FESTIVALS AT EPIPHANY
1. *Night Station at Bethlehem.*[1]

* * * * * * *

Blessed is he that cometh in the Name of the Lord, and the rest which follows.[2] And since, for the sake

[1] The Old Armenian Lectionary of the eighth or ninth century, of which there are two codices with certain variations, one in the Bodleian at Oxford and one at Paris, has preserved for us the antiphons, psalms and lections in use at Jerusalem. They are here given, as far as they bear on Etheria's narrative. At the night station at Bethlehem, Gregory Asharuni, a commentator about 690, mentions that they "assemble in the shepherd's hut" at the ninth hour, and this canon is performed: Ps. xxiii.[1]—[the small [1] here indicates that ver. 1 is sung as an antiphon after each verse of Ps. xxiii.: and so elsewhere]; Alleluiah; Ps. lxxx.; S. Luke ii. 8–20; S. Matt. i. 18–25; Gen. i.–iii. 20; Isa. vii. 10–18; Exod. xiv. 24–xv. 22; Mic. v. 1–8; Prov. i. 1–9; Isa. ix. 5–7; xi. 1–9; xxxv. 4–8; xlii. 1–7; Dan. iii. 1–90; Tit. ii. 11–15; Alleluiah; Ps. cx.; S. Matt. ii. 1–12.

[2] S. Matt. xxi. 9.

of the monks who go on foot, it is necessary to walk slowly, the arrival in Jerusalem thus takes place at the hour when one man begins to be able to recognize another, that is, close upon but a little before daybreak. And on arriving there, the bishop and all with him immediately enter the Anastasis, where an exceedingly great number of lights are already burning. There a psalm is said, prayer is made, first the catechumens and then the faithful are blessed by the bishop; then the bishop retires, and every one returns to his lodging to take rest, but the monks remain there until daybreak and recite hymns.

2. *Morning Services at Jerusalem.*

But after the people have taken rest, at the beginning of the second hour they all assemble in the greater church, which is in Golgotha.[1]

Now it would be superfluous to describe the adornment either of the church, or of the Anastasis, or of the Cross, or in Bethlehem on that day; you see there nothing but gold and gems and silk. For if you look at the veils, they are made wholly of silk striped with gold, and if you look at the curtains, they too are made wholly of silk striped with gold. The church vessels too, of every kind, gold and jewelled, are brought out on that day, and indeed, who could either reckon or describe the number and weight

[1] The Bodleian Codex of the Old Arm. Lect. says that on the second day they assemble in the shrine of S. Stephen, but on the third day they go to the holy shrine in the city (*i.e.* the martyrium, or as Etheria calls it, the greater church in Golgotha), and this canon is prescribed: Ps. cx.³; Heb. i. 1–14; Ps. cx.; S. Matt. ii. 13–23, but Etheria seems to have confused the order of the fourth, fifth and sixth days.

of the *cereofala*,[1] or of the *cicindelae*,[2] or of the *lucernae*,[3] or of the various vessels? And what shall I say of the decoration of the fabric itself, which Constantine, at his mother's instigation, decorated with gold, mosaic, and costly marbles, as far as the resources of his kingdom allowed him, that is, the greater church as well as the Anastasis, at the Cross, and the other holy places in Jerusalem? But to return to the matter in hand: the dismissal[4] takes place on the first day in the greater church, which is in Golgotha, and when they preach or read the several lessons, or recite hymns, all are appropriate to the day. And afterwards when the dismissal from the church has been made, they repair to the Anastasis with hymns, according to custom, so that the dismissal takes place about the sixth hour. And on this day *lucernare* also takes place according to the daily use.

3. *Octave of the Festival.*

On the second day also they proceed in like manner to the church in Golgotha, and also on the third day; thus the feast is celebrated with all this

---

[1] See above, p. 48.

[2] Lamps for burning oil. The word is used four times by S. Gregory of Tours. We also find the expression "*oleum cicindelis*" in the *Life of S. Nicetius, Bishop of Lyons*, and that glass or pottery was probably the material is shown by the following:—"Cicindela—de manibus super lapides lapsa est, quæ nec versa est, nec *fracta*, nec extincta," which occurs in Messianus Presbyter's *Life of S. Cæsarius of Arles*. As late as the twelfth century we still find the word in use. Beroldus was himself a *cicendelarius* at Milan, and fully describes the duty of that functionary.

[3] Lanterns, or lamps.

[4] Here again, although not specified, the Eucharist must have been celebrated.

joyfulness for three days up to the sixth hour in the church built by Constantine. On the fourth[1] day it is celebrated in like manner with similar festal array in Eleona, the very beautiful church which stands on the Mount of Olives; on the fifth day in the Lazarium, which is distant about one thousand five hundred paces from Jerusalem; on the sixth[2] day in Sion, on the seventh[3] day in the Anastasis, and on the eighth day at the Cross. Thus, then, is the feast celebrated with all this joyfulness and festal array throughout the eight days in all the holy places which I have mentioned above. And in Bethlehem also throughout the entire eight days the feast is celebrated with similar festal array and joyfulness daily by the priests and by all the clergy there, and by the monks who are appointed in that place. For from the hour when all return by night to Jerusalem with the bishop, the monks of that place[4] keep vigil in the church in Bethlehem, reciting hymns and antiphons, but it is

[1] On the fourth day the Paris Codex of the Old Arm. Lect. makes the assembly in holy Sion, and this canon is performed: Ps. cx.; Gal. iv. 1–7; Ps. cxxxii.; S. Luke i. 26–38. The fifth day is on the Mount of Olives. Canon: Ps. xcix.; Heb. xii. 18–27; Ps. xv.; S. Luke i. 39–56.

[2] The Paris Codex makes the assembly in the shrine of Lazarus, and they celebrate his raising. Canon: Ps. xxx.; 1 Thess. iv. 12–14; Ps. xl.; S. John xi. 1–46.

[3] The Paris Codex has on the seventh day: "They assemble in holy Golgotha and perform the canon: Ps. xcviii.; Col. ii. 1–15; Alleluiah; Ps. lxxxiv.; S. Luke ii. 21." Here Etheria and the Lectionary again agree, but the Lectionary has not prescribed anything for the eighth day, and it concludes: "Here ends the canon of the Holy Epiphany. By all the martyrs is this canon performed." The later Codex has: "Here ends the canon of the assemblage of holy Epiphany of the Lord. In all commemorations of the holy martyrs this canon is performed."

[4] *i.e.* of Bethlehem,

necessary that the bishop should always keep these days in Jerusalem. And immense crowds, not of monks only, but also of the laity, both men and women, flock together to Jerusalem from every quarter for the solemn and joyous observance of that day.

4. *The Presentation.*[1] *Mass.*

The fortieth day after the Epiphany is undoubtedly celebrated here with the very highest honour, for on that day there is a procession, in which all take part, in the Anastasis, and all things are done in their order with the greatest joy, just as at Easter. All the priests, and after them the bishop, preach, always taking for their subject that part of the Gospel where Joseph and Mary brought the Lord into the Temple on the fortieth day, and Symeon and Anna the prophetess, the daughter of Phanuel, saw Him,—treating of the words which they spake when they saw the Lord, and of that offering which His parents made.[2] And when everything that is customary has been done in order, the sacrament is celebrated, and the dismissal takes place.[3]

---

[1] The Paris Codex gives February 15 as "the Quadragesima of the birth of our Lord Jesus Christ. They assemble in the shrine [*i.e.* martyrium] of the city, and this canon is performed: Ps. xcviii.; *Ktzord* [*i.e.* Antiphon], All the ends . . .; Gal. iii. 24-29; Alleluiah; Ps. xcvi. 2; S. Luke ii. 22-40." The Bodleian Codex has February 14 for this Festival.

[2] S. Luke ii. 22-39.

[3] *Sacramenta aguntur et sic fit missa.*

IV

LENT

And when the Paschal days come they are observed thus:[1] Just as with us forty days are kept before Easter, so here eight weeks are kept before Easter. And eight weeks are kept because there is no fasting on the Lord's Days, nor on the Sabbaths, except on the one Sabbath on which the Vigil of Easter falls, in which case the fast is obligatory. With the exception then of that one day, there is never fasting on any Sabbath here throughout the year. Thus, deducting the eight Lord's Days and the seven Sabbaths (for on the one Sabbath, as I said above, the fast is obligatory) from the eight weeks, there remain forty-one fast days, which they call here *Eortae*, that is *Quadragesimae*.[2]

---

[1] No traces of the Quadragesima are found before the fourth century. The fifth Canon of the Council of Nicæa (325) contains the earliest mention of it. Various endeavours were made in various countries to combine the Quadragesima with Holy Week. S. Chrysostom speaks of the Quadragesima being finished and the "Great week" beginning. At Rome and at Alexandria Holy Week was included in the Quadragesima in such a manner that the whole fast lasted only six weeks, but at Constantinople and in the countries observing the use of Antioch the fast was observed for seven weeks. The Sundays only were excepted at Rome, but at Constantinople both the Sundays and Saturdays, with the exception of Easter Eve, were exempt from fasting.—(Duchesne, *Christian Worship*, 4th edit., pp. 242 f.)

[2] The Old Arm. Lect. has: "For the Holy Quadragesima: first lection, Isa. i. 16-20; second, Ezek. xviii. 20-23; third, Rom. vi. 3-14; fourth, Col. ii. 8 foll.; fifth, Heb. xi. 1-31; sixth, Isa. xlv. 17-26; seventh, Eph. iii. 14-iv. 13; eighth, Jer. xxxii. 19-44; ninth, Job xxxviii. 2-xxxix. 35; tenth, 1 Cor. viii. 5-ix. 23; eleventh, Heb. i. 1-12; twelfth, Isa. vii. 11-vii. 10; thirteenth, Isa. liii. 1-liv. 5; fourteenth, 1 Cor. xv. 1-28

1. *Services on Sundays.*

Now the several days of the several weeks are kept thus :

On the Lord's Day after the first cockcrow the bishop reads in the Anastasis the account of the Lord's Resurrection from the Gospel, as on all Lord's Days throughout the whole year, and everything is done at the Anastasis and at the Cross as on all Lord's Days throughout the year, up to daybreak. Afterwards, in the morning, they proceed to the greater church, called the martyrium, which is in Golgotha behind the Cross, and all things that are customary on the Lord's Days are done there. In like manner also when the dismissal from the church has been made, they go with hymns to the Anastasis, as they always do on the Lord's Days, and while these things are being done the fifth hour is reached. *Lucernare*, however, takes place at its own hour, as usual, at the Anastasis and at the Cross, and in the various holy places ; on the Lord's Day the ninth hour is [1] kept.

2. *Weekday Services.*

On the second weekday they go at the first cockcrow to the Anastasis, as they do throughout the year, and everything that is usual is done until morning. Then at the third hour they go to the

---

fifteenth, Dan. vii. 13-27 ; sixteenth, 1 Cor. xii. 1-7 ; seventeenth, 1 Cor. xii. 8-27 ; eighteenth, Ezek. xxxvii. 1-14 ; nineteenth, 1 Tim. iii. 14-16. Here ends the canon of them that are going to be baptized."

[1] Mgr. Duchesne would here insert "not."

Anastasis, and the things are done that are customary throughout the year at the sixth hour, for this going at the third hour in Quadragesima is additional. At the sixth and ninth hours also, and at *lucernare*, everything is done that is customary throughout the whole year at the holy places. And on the third weekday all things are done as on the second weekday.

3. *Wednesday and Friday.*

Again, on the fourth [1] weekday they go by night to the Anastasis, and all the usual things are done until morning, and also at the third and sixth hours. But at the ninth hour they go to Sion, as is customary at that hour on the fourth and sixth [2] weekdays throughout the year, for the reason that the fast is always kept here on the fourth and sixth weekdays even by the catechumens, except a martyrs' day should occur. For if a martyrs' day should chance to occur on the fourth or on the sixth weekday in Quadragesima, they do not go to Sion at the ninth hour. But on the days of Quadragesima, as I said above, they proceed to Sion on the fourth weekday at the ninth hour, according to the custom of the whole year, and all things that are customary at the ninth hour are done, except the oblation, for, in order that the

[1] The Old Arm. Lect. has: "In the holy Quadragesima, in the first week on the fourth day of the week, they assemble at the tenth hour in holy Sion, and this canon is performed: Exod. i. 1–ii. 10; Joel i. 14–20; Ps. li. 5 ff." (Gregory Asharuni alone gives the fifth verse as the antiphon.)

[2] The Old Arm. Lect.: "Friday, at the tenth hour they assemble in holy Sion, and this canon is performed: Deut. vi. 4–vii. 10; Job vi. 2–vii. 13; Isa. xl. 1–8; Ps. xli.[4]"

people may always be instructed in the law, both the bishop and the priest preach diligently. But when the dismissal has been made, the people escort the bishop with hymns thence to the Anastasis, so that it is already the hour of *lucernare* when he enters the Anastasis; then hymns and antiphons are said, prayers are made, and the service (*missa*) of *lucernare* takes place in the Anastasis and at the Cross. And the service of *lucernare* is always later on those days in Quadragesima than on other days throughout the year. On the fifth weekday everything is done as on the second and third weekday. On the sixth weekday everything is done as on the fourth, including the going to Sion at the ninth hour, and the escorting of the bishop thence to the Anastasis with hymns.

4. *Saturday.*

But on the sixth weekday the vigils are observed in the Anastasis from the hour of their arrival from Sion with hymns, until morning, that is, from the hour of *lucernare*, when they entered, to the morning of the next day, that is, the Sabbath. And the oblation is made in the Anastasis the earlier, that the dismissal may take place before sunrise. Throughout the whole night psalms are said responsively in turn with antiphons and with various lections, the whole lasting until morning, and the dismissal, which takes place on the Sabbath at the Anastasis, is before sunrise, that is, the oblation, so that the dismissal may take place in the Anastasis at the hour when the sun begins to rise. Thus, then, is each week of Quadragesima kept, the dismissal taking place earlier on the Sabbath, *i.e.* before sunrise, as I said, in order that the *hebdomadarii*, as they are called here, may finish their fast earlier. For the custom of the fast in Quadragesima is that the dismissal on the Lord's Day is at the fifth hour in order that they whom they call *hebdomadarii*, that is, they who keep the weeks' fast, may take food. And when these have taken breakfast on the Lord's Day, they do not eat until the Sabbath morning after they have communicated in the Anastasis. It is for their sake, then, that they may finish their fast the sooner, that the dismissal on the Sabbath at the Anastasis is before sunrise. For their sake the dismissal is in the morning, as I said; not that they alone communicate, but all who are so minded communicate on that day in the Anastasis.

5. *The Fast.*

This is the custom of the fast in Quadragesima: some, when they have eaten after the dismissal on the Lord's Day, that is, about the fifth or sixth hour, do not eat throughout the whole week until after the dismissal at the Anastasis on the Sabbath; these are they who keep the weeks' fast.

Nor, after having eaten in the morning, do they eat in the evening of the Sabbath, but they take a meal on the next day, that is, on the Lord's Day, after the dismissal from the church at the fifth hour or later, and then they do not breakfast until the Sabbath comes round, as I have said above. For the custom here is that all who are *apotactitae*, as they call them here, whether men or women, eat only once a day on the day when they do eat, not only in Quadragesima, but throughout the whole year. But if any of the *apotactitae* cannot keep the entire week of fasting as described above, they take supper in the middle (of the week), on the fifth day, all through Quadragesima. And if any one cannot do even this, he keeps two days' fast (in the week) all through Quadragesima, and they who cannot do even this, take a meal every evening. For no one exacts from any how much he should do, but each does what he can, nor is he praised who has done much, nor is he blamed who has done less; that is the custom here. For their food during the days of Quadragesima is as follows:—they taste neither bread which cannot be weighed,[1] nor oil, nor anything that grows on trees, but only water and a little gruel made of flour. Quadragesima is kept thus, as we have said. And at the end of the weeks' fast the vigil is kept in the Anastasis from the hour of *lucernare* on the sixth weekday, when the people come with psalms from Sion, to the morning of the Sabbath, when the oblation is made in the Anastasis. And the second, third, fourth, fifth and sixth weeks in Quadragesima are kept as the first.[2]

[1] *Panem, quid liberari non potest*, but Archbp. Bernard reads *qui deliquari* and translates: "bread which cannot be strained as a liquid." I have adopted Gamurrini's conjecture *librari*.

[2] In the Old Arm. Lect. there are special lections for all these weeks. They will be found in the *Rituale Armenorum*, Appendix II., pp. 519 f. As they do not specially figure in Etheria's narrative, they are not given here. The places of assembly in Jerusalem are specified with each day's lections.

V

HOLY WEEK AND THE FESTIVALS AT EASTER

1. *Saturday before Palm Sunday.—Station at Bethany.*

Now when the seventh week has come, that is, when two weeks, including the seventh, are left before Easter,[1] everything is done on each day as in the weeks that are past, except that the vigils of the sixth weekday, which were kept in the Anastasis during the first six weeks, are, in the seventh week, kept in Sion, and with the same customs that obtained during the six weeks in the Anastasis. For throughout the whole vigil psalms and antiphons are said appropriate both to the place and to the day.

And when the morning of the Sabbath[2] begins to dawn, the bishop offers the oblation. And at the dismissal the archdeacon lifts his voice and says: "Let us all be ready to-day at the seventh hour in the Lazarium." And so, as the seventh hour approaches, all go to the Lazarium, that is, Bethany, situated at about the second milestone from the city. And as they go from Jerusalem to the Lazarium, there is, about five hundred paces from the latter place, a church in the street on that spot where Mary the

---

[1] Mgr. Duchesne notes there were variations in the length of the Quadragesima at Jerusalem (*Christian Worship*, p. 243, note 4, 4th edit.). The Old Arm. Lect. reckons Holy Week as the seventh, and Etheria the eighth of Quadragesima. The meeting-places also do not quite agree in the two MSS.

[2] For the Saturday before Palm Sunday the Old Arm. Lect. gives: "The sixth day before Zatik (the Passover), on the Sabbath they assemble in the Lazarium, and this canon is performed: Ps. xxx.³; 1 Thess. iv. 12-17; Alleluiah; Ps. xl.; S. John xi. 55-xii. 11."

sister of Lazarus met with the Lord.¹ Here, when the bishop arrives, all the monks meet him, and the people enter the church, and one hymn and one antiphon are said, and that passage is read in the Gospel where the sister of Lazarus meets the Lord. Then, after prayer has been made, and when all have been blessed, they go thence with hymns to the Lazarium. And on arriving at the Lazarium, so great a multitude assembles that not only the place itself, but also the fields around, are full of people. Hymns and antiphons suitable to the day and to the place are said, and likewise all the lessons are read. Then, before the dismissal, notice is given of Easter, that is, the priest ascends to a higher place and reads the passage that is written in the Gospel: *When Jesus six days before the Passover had come to Bethany*, and the rest.² So, that passage having been read and notice given of Easter, the dismissal is made. This is done on that day because, as it is written in the Gospel, these events took place in Bethany six days before the Passover; there being six days from the Sabbath to the fifth weekday on which, after supper, the Lord was taken by night. Then all return to the city direct to the Anastasis, and *lucernare* takes place according to custom.

2. *Palm Sunday.*—(*a*) *Services in the Churches.*

On the next day, that is, the Lord's Day,³ which

[1] S. John xi. 29, 30.   [2] S. John xii. 1 ff.
[3] The Old Arm. Lect. has: "On the Day of the Palms they assemble in the holy Shrine of the city, and this canon is fulfilled: Ps. xcviii. 8; Eph. i. 3-10; Alleluiah; Ps. xcix.; S. Matt. xxi. 1-11."

begins the Paschal week, and which they call here the Great Week, when all the customary services from cockcrow until morning have taken place in the Anastasis and at the Cross, they proceed on the morning of the Lord's Day according to custom to the greater church which is called the martyrium. It is called the martyrium because it is in Golgotha behind the Cross, where the Lord suffered. When all that is customary has been observed in the great church, and before the dismissal is made, the archdeacon lifts his voice and says first : "Throughout the whole week, beginning from to-morrow, let us all assemble in the martyrium, that is, in the great church, at the ninth hour." Then he lifts his voice again, saying : "Let us all be ready to-day in Eleona at the seventh hour." So when the dismissal has been made in the great church, that is, the martyrium, the bishop is escorted with hymns to the Anastasis, and after all things that are customary on the Lord's Day have been done there, after the dismissal from the martyrium, every one hastens home to eat, that all may be ready at the beginning of the seventh hour in the church in Eleona, on the Mount of Olives, where is the cave in which the Lord was wont to teach.

(*b*) *Procession with Palms on the Mount of Olives.*

Accordingly at the seventh hour [1] all the people

[1] The Old Arm. Lect. has : "On the same day, at the ninth hour, they go forth to the Mount of Olives with palm branches ; and there they pray and sing psalms until the tenth hour. And after that they go down into the holy Anastasis, chanting Ps. cxviii.[26]" [N.B.—This psalm formed part of the Jewish

go up to the Mount of Olives, that is, to Eleona, and the bishop with them, to the church, where hymns and antiphons suitable to the day and to the place are said, and lessons in like manner. And when the ninth hour approaches they go up with hymns to the Imbomon, that is, to the place whence the Lord ascended into heaven, and there they sit down, for all the people are always bidden to sit when the bishop is present; the deacons alone always stand. Hymns and antiphons suitable to the day and to the place are said, interspersed with lections and prayers. And as the eleventh hour approaches, the passage from the Gospel is read, where the children, carrying branches and palms, met the Lord, saying; *Blessed is He that cometh in the name of the Lord*,[1] and the bishop immediately rises, and all the people with him, and they all go on foot from the top of the Mount of Olives, all the people going before him with hymns and antiphons, answering one to another: *Blessed is He that cometh in the Name of the Lord.* And all the children in the neighbourhood, even those who are too young to walk, are carried by their parents on their shoulders, all of them bearing branches, some of palms and some of olives,[2] and thus the bishop is escorted in the same manner as the Lord was of old. For all, even those of rank, both matrons and men, accompany the bishop all the way on foot in this manner, making these

---

Hallel. It will be observed that Etheria's ear caught the ever-recurring antiphon: "Blessed is He that cometh in the name of the Lord" (v. 26), but she does not seem to have recognized the psalm. According to the ancient use, the antiphon was sung after each verse as a refrain.]

[1] S. Matt. xxi. 9. [2] S. Matt. xxi. 8.

responses, from the top of the mount to the city, and thence through the whole city to the Anastasis, going very slowly lest the people should be wearied; and thus they arrive at the Anastasis at a late hour. And on arriving, although it is late, *lucernare* takes place, with prayer at the Cross; after which the people are dismissed.

3. *Monday in Holy Week.*

On the next day, the second weekday, everything that is customary is done from the first cockcrow until morning in the Anastasis; also at the third and sixth hours everything is done that is customary throughout the whole of Quadragesima. But at the ninth hour all assemble in the great church, that is the martyrium,[1] where hymns and antiphons are said continuously until the first hour of the night and lessons suitable to the day and the place are read, interspersed always with prayers. *Lucernare* takes place when its hour approaches, that is, so that it is already night when the dismissal at the martyrium is made. When the dismissal has been made, the bishop is escorted thence with hymns to the Anastasis, where, when he has entered, one hymn is said, followed by a prayer; the catechumens and then the faithful are blessed, and the dismissal is made.

[1] The Old Arm. Lect. has: "The second day of the week of the Fast of Zatik (Pascha) they assemble in the holy Shrine of the city, and this canon is fulfilled: Gen. i. 1–iii. 20; Prov. i. 1–9; Isa. xl. 1–8; Ps. lxv.[5]"

4. *Tuesday in Holy Week.*

On the third weekday[1] everything is done as on the second, with this one thing added—that late at night, after the dismissal of the martyrium, and after the going to the Anastasis and after the dismissal there, all proceed at that hour by night to the church, which is on the mount Eleona. And when they have arrived at that church, the bishop enters the cave where the Lord was wont to teach His disciples,[2] and after receiving the book of the Gospel, he stands and himself reads the words of the Lord which are written in the Gospel according to Matthew, where He says: *Take heed that no man deceive you.*[3] And the bishop reads through the whole of that discourse, and when he has read it, prayer is made, the catechumens and the faithful are blessed, the dismissal is made, and every one returns from the mount to his house, it being already very late at night.

5. *Wednesday in Holy Week.*

On the fourth weekday everything is done as on the second and third weekdays throughout the whole day from the first cockcrow onwards, but after the dismissal has taken place at the martyrium[4] by night,

---

[1] The Old Arm. Lect. has: "On the third day of the week [the later Bodleian Codex has: 'they assemble on the Mount of Olives,' thus agreeing with Etheria], at the tenth hour. And this canon is performed: Gen. vi. 9–ix. 17; Prov. ix. 1–11; Isa. xi. 9–17; Ps. xxv.[1]; S. Matt. xxiv. 3–xxvi. 3."

[2] Cf. S. Matt. xxiv. 3.   [3] S. Matt. xxiv. 4.

[4] The old Arm. Lect. has: "The fourth day of the week at the tenth hour they assemble in the holy Shrine of the city, and this canon is performed: Gen. xviii. 1–xix. 30; Prov. i.

THE PILGRIMAGE OF ETHERIA 69

and the bishop has been escorted with hymns to the Anastasis, he at once enters the cave which is in the Anastasis, and stands within the rails; but the priest stands before the rails and receives the Gospel, and reads the passage where Judas Iscariot went to the Jews and stated what they should give him that he should betray the Lord.[1] And when the passage has been read, there is such a moaning and groaning of all the people that no one can help being moved to tears at that hour. Afterwards prayer follows, then the blessing, first of the catechumens, and then of the faithful, and the dismissal is made.

6. *Maundy Thursday.*—(a) *Mass celebrated twice.*

On the fifth weekday everything that is customary is done from the first cockcrow until morning at the Anastasis, and also at the third and at the sixth hours. But at the eighth hour all the people gather together at the martyrium [2] according to custom, only

---

10–19; Zech. xi. 11–14; Ps. xli.[4] And after the psalm they go down into the holy Anastasis, and a lection is read, S. Matt. xxvi. 14–16."

[1] S. Matt. xxvi. 14, 15.

[2] The Old Arm. Lect. has: "The fifth day of the week is of the old Zatik, as touching which Jesus said to His disciples, 'With desire have I desired to eat with you this Zatik.' They assemble at the seventh hour in the holy shrine of the city, and this canon is performed: Gen. xxii. 1–18; Isa. lxi. 1–6; Acts i. 15–26; Ps. lv.[22] *Their words*, etc. Then the catechumens are dismissed. Again Is. xxiii.[5]; 1 Cor. xi. 23–33; S. Matt. xxvi. 20–39.

And then the sacrifice is offered in the holy shrine, and before the holy Cross. And in the same hour they proceed to holy Sion. The canon and Apostle are the same: For I received from the Lord: S. Mark xiv. 12–26.

And in the same hour they go forth to the Mount of Olives, and perform the evening service of worship. And they join

earlier than on other days, because the dismissal must be made sooner. Then, when the people are gathered together, all that should be done is done, and the oblation is made on that day at the martyrium, the dismissal taking place about the tenth hour. But before the dismissal is made there, the archdeacon raises his voice and says: "Let us all assemble at the first hour of the night in the church which is in Eleona, for great toil awaits us to-day, in this very night." Then, after the dismissal at the martyrium, they arrive behind the Cross, where only one hymn is said and prayer is made, and the bishop offers the oblation there, and all communicate. Nor is the oblation ever offered behind the Cross on any day throughout the year, except on this one day. And after the dismissal

---

with the same the vigil, and with three *gubalays* of psalms. [Mr. Conybeare believes *gubalay* to be derived from κεφαλαιον = chapter. Each canon of the psalms is divided for liturgical purposes into seven *gubalays*, each *gubalay* comprising two or three Psalms, and at the end of it is repeated the *Gloria Patri*.] And the prayers are said with *gonuklisia* [genuflections].

Of the first *gubalay*, Ps. ii.[2]
Of the second *gubalay*, Ps. xli.[5]
Of the third *gubalay*, Ps. lix.[1]
Of the fourth *gubalay*, Ps. lxxxviii.[5], *Ktzord*, They are cut off from thy hand.
Of the fifth *gubalay*, Ps. cix[2]., *Ktzord*, They spake of me and with deceitful tongue.

And after the fifth Psalm, and fifth *gubalay*, and fifth prayer, on the same evening they read the Gospel of S. John xiii. 31–xviii. 1.

On the same evening they go up to the hillock [on the Mt. of Olives. The Bordeaux pilgrim calls it 'the little hill.' Sir C. Wilson thinks it may be the slight elevation on the ridge of Olivet, known afterwards as Galilee], and this canon is performed: Ps. cix.[4]; S. Luke xxii. 39–46.

In the same hour of night they assemble in the room of the disciples, and read the lection, S. Mark xiv. 33–42."

there they go to the Anastasis, where prayer is made, the catechumens and the faithful are blessed according to custom, and the dismissal is made.

(b) *Night Station on the Mount of Olives.*

And so every one hastens back to his house to eat, because immediately after they have eaten, all go to Eleona to the church wherein is the cave where the Lord was with His Apostles on this very day. There then, until about the fifth hour of the night, hymns and antiphons suitable to the day and to the place are said, lessons, too, are read in like manner, with prayers interspersed, and the passages from the Gospel are read where the Lord addressed His disciples on that same day as He sat in the same cave which is in that church. And they go thence at about the sixth hour of the night with hymns up to the Imbomon, the place whence the Lord ascended into heaven, where again lessons are read, hymns and antiphons suitable to the day are said, and all the prayers which are made by the bishop are also suitable both to the day and to the place.

(c) *Stations at Gethsemane.*

And at the first cockcrow they come down from the Imbomon with hymns, and arrive at the place where the Lord prayed, as it is written in the Gospel[1]: *and He was withdrawn*[2] (*from them*) *about a stone's cast, and prayed,* and the rest. There is in that place a graceful church. The bishop and all the people

[1] S. Luke xxii. 41.
[2] Lat. *et accessit*, but Vulg. has *ipse avulsus est*, see p. xxxiv.

enter, a prayer suitable to the place and to the day is said, with one suitable hymn, and the passage from the Gospel is read where He said to His disciples: *Watch, that ye enter not into temptation*[1]; the whole passage is read through and prayer is made. And then all, even to the smallest child, go down with the Bishop, on foot, with hymns to Gethsemane; where, on account of the great number of people in the crowd, who are wearied owing to the vigils and weak through the daily fasts, and because they have so great a hill to descend, they come very slowly with hymns to Gethsemane. And over two hundred church candles are made ready to give light to all the people. On their arrival at Gethsemane,[2] first a suitable prayer is made, then a hymn is said, then the passage of the Gospel is read where the Lord was taken. And when this passage has been read there is so great a moaning and groaning of all the people, together with weeping, that their lamentation may be heard perhaps as far as the city.

(*d*) *Return to Jerusalem.*

From that hour they go with hymns[3] to the city on foot, reaching the gate about the time when one man begins to be able to recognize another, and thence right on through the midst of the city; all, to a man, both great and small, rich and poor, all are ready

---

[1] S. Mark xiv. 38.

[2] The Old Arm. Lit. has: "In the same hour of night, in the holy Mount of Olives in Gethsemane. And they read S. Matt. xxvi. 36–56."

[3] The Old Arm. Lit. has: "In the same hour of night they come singing Ps. cxviii.¹, and they recite it until they come before Golgotha, and he reads S. Matt. xxvi. 57–xxvii. 2."

there, for on that special day not a soul withdraws from the vigils until morning. Thus the bishop is escorted from Gethsemane to the gate, and thence through the whole of the city to the Cross.

7. *Good Friday.*—(*a*) *Service at Daybreak.*

And when they arrive before the Cross the daylight is already growing bright. There the passage from the Gospel is read where the Lord is brought before Pilate, with everything that is written concerning that which Pilate spake to the Lord or to the Jews;[1] the whole is read. And afterwards the bishop addresses the people, comforting them for that they have toiled all night and are about to toil during that same day, (bidding) them not be weary, but to have hope in God, Who will for that toil give them a greater reward. And encouraging them as he is able, he addresses them thus: "Go now, each one of you, to your houses, and sit down awhile, and all of you be ready here just before the second hour of the day, that from that hour to the sixth you may be able to behold the holy wood of the Cross, each one of us believing that it will be profitable to his salvation; then from the sixth hour we must all assemble again in this place, that is, before the Cross, that we may apply ourselves to lections and to prayers until night."

(*b*) *The Column of the Flagellation.*

After this, when the dismissal at the Cross has been made, that is, before the sun rises, they all go

[1] S. Matt. xxvii. 2, etc.; S. Mark xv. 1, etc.; S. Luke xxiii. 1, etc.; S. John xviii. 28, etc.

at once with fervour to Sion, to pray at the column at which the Lord was scourged.[1] And returning thence they sit for awhile in their houses, and presently all are ready.

(c) *Veneration of the Cross.*

Then a chair is placed for the bishop in Golgotha[2] behind the Cross, which is now standing;[3] the bishop duly takes his seat in the chair, and a table covered with a linen cloth is placed before him; the deacons stand round the table, and a silver-gilt casket is

---

[1] The Old Arm. Lit. has: "In the same hour of the night they go to the palace of the Judge, and he [*i.e.* the Lector] reads S. John xviii. 28–xix. 16."

[2] The Old Arm. Lit. has: "At dawn, on the Friday, the holy wood of the cross is set before holy Golgotha, and the congregation adore until the ninth hour. The adoration is completed, and at the sixth hour they assemble in holy Golgotha, and repeat eight psalms and five Gospel lections. And one by one of the psalms, there are two and lections, and at the same time prayers.

Ps. xxxv. 11. [It is not easy to understand this, but Mr. Conybeare thinks the arrangement was thus: Ps. standing for Psalm, and L. for Lection: L. Ps. Ps. L. Ps. Ps. L. Ps. Ps. L. Ps. Ps. L., making five Lections and eight Psalms.]

Lection i.: Zech. xi. 11–14; Gal. vi. 14–18; Ps. xxxviii.[17]; Isa. iii. 9–15; Phil. ii. 5–11.

Prayer with *gonuklisia* [genuflection] Ps. xli.[6]; Isa. l. 4–9; Rom. v. 6–11; Alleluiah; Ps. xxii. 18; Amos viii. 9–12; 1 Cor. i. 18–31.

Prayer with *gonuklisia*: Ps. xxxi.[5]; Isa. lii. 13–liii.[12]; Heb. ii. 11–18; S. Matt. xxvii. 3–53; Heb. ix. 11–28; S. Mark (in MS. Matt.) xv. 16–41.

Prayer with *gonuklisia*: Ps. lxxxviii.[4] Lection xiii: Jer. (in MS. Isa.) xi. 18–21; Heb. x. 19–31; S. Luke xxiii. 32–(49). [The folio being torn, the part within brackets ( ) is added from the Bodleian MS. and so on the next line.].

(Prayer with *gonuklisia*. Ps. cii.[1]; Zech. xiv. 6–)11; Lection xvi.; 1 Tim. vi. 13–16; S. John xix. 25–37."

[3] See Introduction, p. xlv.

brought in which is the holy wood of the Cross. The casket is opened and (the wood) is taken out, and both the wood of the Cross and the title [1] are placed upon the table. Now, when it has been put upon the table, the bishop, as he sits, holds the extremities of the sacred wood firmly in his hands, while the deacons who stand around guard it. It is guarded thus because the custom is that the people, both faithful and catechumens, come one by one and, bowing down at the table, kiss the sacred wood and pass through. And because, I know not when, some one is said to have bitten off and stolen a portion of the sacred wood, it is thus guarded by the deacons who stand around, lest any one approaching should venture to do so again. And as all the people pass by one by one, all bowing themselves, they touch the Cross and the title, first with their foreheads and then with their eyes; then they kiss the Cross and pass through, but none lays his hand upon it to touch it. When they have kissed the Cross and have passed through, a deacon stands holding the ring of Solomon and the horn from which the kings were anointed; they kiss the horn also and gaze at the ring [2] . . . all the

[1] Rufinus, *Hist. Eccl.* i. 7, 8 (about 400), is responsible for the statement that part of the wood of the true cross was sent to Constantine and part left in a silver casket (as here) in Jerusalem. According to S. Ambrose (395) Pilate's original superscription (*titulus*) was found by Helena still attached to the Saviour's cross, which enabled her to distinguish it from the two others; but other authorities, including Rufinus, state that it was found in a separate place from the cross, and that the recognition of the true cross was due to a miracle. Evidently at the time of Etheria's visit the "title" was shown as one of the relics at Jerusalem.

[2] There is here an hiatus in the MS., with the two untranslatable words *minus secunda* in the middle.

people are passing through up to the sixth hour, entering by one door and going out by another; for this is done in the same place where, on the preceding day, that is, on the fifth weekday, the oblation was offered.

(*d*) *Station before the Cross. The Three Hours.*

And when the sixth hour has come, they go before the Cross, whether it be in rain or in heat, the place being open to the air, as it were, a court of great size and of some beauty between the Cross and the Anastasis; here all the people assemble in such great numbers that there is no thoroughfare. The chair is placed for the bishop before the Cross, and from the sixth to the ninth hour nothing else is done, but the reading of lessons, which are read thus: first from the psalms wherever the Passion is spoken of, then from the Apostle, either from the epistles of the Apostles or from their Acts, wherever they have spoken of the Lord's Passion; then the passages from the Gospels, where He suffered, are read. Then the readings from the prophets where they foretold that the Lord should suffer, then from the Gospels where He mentions His Passion. Thus from the sixth to the ninth hours the lessons are so read and the hymns said, that it may be shown to all the people that whatsoever the prophets foretold of the Lord's Passion is proved from the Gospels and from the writings of the Apostles to have been fulfilled. And so through all those three hours the people are taught that nothing was done which had not been foretold, and that nothing was foretold which was not wholly fulfilled. Prayers also suitable to the day are interspersed throughout. The emotion shown and the mourning by all the people at every lesson and prayer is wonderful; for there is none, either great or small, who, on that day during those three hours, does not lament more than can be conceived, that the Lord had suffered those things for us.[1]

Afterwards, at the beginning of the ninth hour, there is read that passage from the Gospel according to John where He gave up the ghost.[2] This read, prayer and the dismissal follow.

(e) Evening Offices.

And when the dismissal before the Cross has been made, all things are done in the greater church, at the martyrium, which are customary during this week from the ninth hour [3]—when the assembly takes place in the martyrium—until late. And after the dismissal at the martyrium, they go to the Anastasis, where, when they arrive, the passage from the Gospel is read where Joseph begged the Body of the Lord from Pilate and laid it in a new sepulchre.[4] And this reading ended, a prayer is said, the catechumens are blessed, and the dismissal is made.

But on that day no announcement is made of a

[1] This is probably the earliest record we have of the observance of the "Three Hours."

[2] S. John xix. 30.

[3] The Old Arm. Lect. has: "Prayer with *gonuklisia*. And then they go up into the church at the tenth hour. [The later Bodleian MS. in the place of "church" says "holy shrine," which agrees with Etheria's "martyrium"]. And this canon is performed: Jer. xi. 18–20. Lection xvii.; Isa. liii. 1–12; Ps. xxii.[18]; S. Matt. xxvii. 57–61."

[4] S. John xix. 38–42.

vigil at the Anastasis, because it is known that the people are tired; nevertheless, it is the custom to watch there. So all of the people who are willing, or rather, who are able, keep watch, and they who are unable do not watch there until the morning. Those of the clergy, however, who are strong or young keep vigil there, and hymns and antiphons are said throughout the whole night until morning; a very great crowd also keep night-long watch, some from the late hour and some from midnight, as they are able.

8. *Vigil of Easter.*

Now, on the next day, the Sabbath,[1] everything that

---

[1] The Old Arm. Lect. has: "On the Sabbath day at dawn, in the holy Anastasis: Ps. lxxxviii. 6; S. Matt. xxvii. 62–66.

At eventide, on the Sabbath day, they light a torch in the holy Anastasis.

First the bishop repeats Ps. cxiii.[2] And then the bishop lights three candles; and after him the deacons, and then the whole congregation. And then, after that, they go up into the church [the martyrium] and begin the vigils of the holy Zatik [Paschal vigils, as Etheria calls them], and read twelve lections. And with each of them they sing psalms. [Here is evidently the primitive form of the ceremony of the New Fire in the ritual of the Greek Church at Jerusalem, to which such importance is still attached. The ceremony does not, however, extend beyond the Holy City, and it was not known at Rome. Etheria seems to have missed this service of the lighting of the candles: her narrative is concentrated on the newly baptized. There is no mention in the Old Arm. Lect. or in Etheria's narrative of the blessing of the Paschal candle, which was an ancient custom in N. Italy, Gaul and Spain, and perhaps Africa. Cf. Duchesne, *Christian Worship*, pp. 251 f.].

Prayers with *gonuklisia:* Ps. cxviii.[24]; Gen. i. 1–iii. 24: Gen. xxii. 1–18; Exod. xii. 1–24; Jonah i. 1–iv. 11; Exod. xiv. 24–xv. 21; Isa. lx. 1–13.

[This lection is farced verse by verse with the respond: 'Behold, there is come the King of Glory of light, illumining all creatures'].

THE PILGRIMAGE OF ETHERIA

is customary is done at the third hour and also at the sixth; the service at the ninth hour, however, is not held on the Sabbath, but the Paschal vigils are prepared in the great church, the martyrium. The Paschal vigils are kept as with us, with this one addition, that the children when they have been baptised and clothed, and when they issue from the font,[1] are led with the bishop first to the Anastasis; the bishop enters the rails of the Anastasis, and one hymn is said, then the bishop says a prayer for them, and then he goes with them to the greater church,

---

Prayers with *gonuklisia*: Job xxxviii. 1–28; 4 Kings (2 Kings) ii. 1–22; Jer. xxxi. 31–34; Josh. i. 1–9; Ezek. xxxvii. 1–14; Dan. iii. 1–90, LXX. [See the Song of the Three Holy Children in the Apocrypha.]

[This is farced at v. 33 after the words: 'Take not thy mercy away from us,' with the respond, written in small uncials: 'The incorruptible Holy Trinity has beamed forth on us from incorruptible light. And do thou work propitiatory mercy; for thee alone do we know to be our Saviour.' Again, at v. 52, after the words: 'They glorified God in the midst of the furnace, and said,' comes the respond: 'The ram of Isaac hath been exchanged. Christ is become unto us for salvation.'

In the rest of the hymn the words: 'Praise and exalt Him for ever,' are repeated thirty times, as a respond after each verse.]

And while they recite the hymn, in the middle of the night, there enter the multitude of the deacons [the Bodleian MS. gives 'newly sealed.' N.B.—The Old Arm. Lect. seems to give two processional entries to the martyrium from the Anastasis. One, when they begin the 'vigils of the holy Zatik,' and one with the newly baptized. Etheria seems to give merely the latter. Section 8, 'Vigil of Easter'] together with the bishop, and this canon is performed: Ps. lxv.[1] Lection; 1 Cor. xv. 1–11; Alleluiah; Ps. xxx.[1]; S. Matt. xxviii. 1–20."

[1] *i.e.* in the baptistery which Constantine had built beside the church of the Anastasis. The rite was one of total immersion, and many of the catechumens were adults (Archbp. Bernard), although Etheria uses the word *infantes* of them here: see Thompson on *Baptismal Offices*, p. 177.

proceed) to the great church again, that is, to the martyrium.

Moreover, on the eight Paschal days the bishop goes every day after breakfast up to Eleona with all the clergy, and with all the children who have been baptised, and with all who are *apotactitae*, both men and women, and likewise with all the people who are willing. Hymns are said and prayers are made, both in the church which is on Eleona, wherein is the cave where Jesus was wont to teach His disciples, and also in the Imbomon, that is, in the place whence the Lord ascended into heaven. And when the psalms have been said and prayer has been made, they come down thence with hymns to the Anastasis at the hour of *lucernare*. This is done throughout all the eight days.

10. *Vesper Station at Sion on Easter Sunday.*[1]

Now, on the Lord's Day at Easter, after the dismissal of *lucernare*, that is, at the Anastasis, all the people escort the bishop with hymns to Sion. And, on arriving, hymns suitable to the day and place are said, prayer is made, and the passage from the Gospel

---

directly on any part of Etheria's narrative, but are given here because they bear on the administration of the Mysteries:

"Lections of the administration of the Mystery ($=\mu\nu\sigma\tau\alpha\gamma\omega\gamma\iota\alpha$) after the dismissal are [read] in the shrine on the second day in the same week: 1 Pet. v. 8–14.

Next he administers the Mystery on the seventh day in the same week: 1 Cor. xi. 23–32.

The Sunday at the close of *Zatik*. He reads in the holy Anastasis during the administration of the Mystery: 1 Pet. ii. 1–10."

[N.B. The lections given in S. Cyril's *Catech. Orat.* seem to tally in general with this whole series.]

[1] See note 1 on preceding page.

is read where the Lord,[1] on the same day, and in the same place where the church now stands in Sion, came in to His disciples when the doors were shut. That is, when one of His disciples, Thomas, was absent, and when he returned and the other Apostles told him that they had seen the Lord, he said: "*Except I shall see, I will not believe.*"[2] When this has been read, prayer is again made, the catechumens and the faithful are blessed, and every one returns to his house late, about the second hour of the night.

11. *Sunday after Easter.*

Again, on the Octave of Easter,[3] that is, on the Lord's Day, all the people go up to Eleona with the bishop immediately after the sixth hour. First they sit for awhile in the church which is there, and hymns and antiphons suitable to the day and to the place are said; prayers suitable to the day and to the place are likewise made. Then they go up to the Imbomon with hymns, and the same things are done there as in the former place. And when the time comes, all the people and all the *apotactitae* escort the bishop with hymns down to the Anastasis, arriving there at the usual hour for *lucernare*. So *lucernare* takes place at the Anastasis and at the Cross, and all the people to a man escort the bishop thence with hymns to Sion. And when they have arrived, hymns suitable to the day and to the place are said there also, and lastly that passage from the Gospel is read where,

[1] S. John xx. 19.   [2] S. John xx. 25.
[3] See note 4 on page 81. "On the same Sunday," etc.

on the Octave of Easter,[1] the Lord came in where the disciples were, and reproved Thomas because he had been unbelieving. The whole of that lesson is read, with prayer afterwards; both the catechumens and the faithful are blessed, and every one returns to his house as usual, just as on the Lord's Day of Easter, at the second hour of the night.

12. *Easter to Whitsuntide.*

Now, from Easter to the fiftieth day, that is, to Pentecost, no one fasts here, not even those who are *apotactitae*. During these days, as throughout the whole year, the customary things are done at the Anastasis from the first cockcrow until morning, and at the sixth hour and at *lucernare* likewise. But on the Lord's Days the procession is always to the martyrium, that is, to the great church, according to custom, and they go thence with hymns to the Anastasis. On the fourth and sixth weekdays, as no one fasts during those days, the procession is to Sion, but in the morning; the dismissal is made in its due order.

13. *The Ascension.—Festival at Bethlehem.*[2]

On the fortieth day after Easter, that is, on the fifth

---

[1] S. John xx. 26–29.

[2] Between Easter and Whitsunday Etheria describes no festivals with the exception of this cursory mention of the Ascension, of which "it is impossible to find a trace before the middle of the fourth century" (Duchesne). It is not given in the Old Arm. Lect., but on May 7 we find the following—

"They assemble before holy Golgotha, on the day of the appearance in heaven of the Sign of the holy Cross, and this weekday—(for all go on the previous day, that is, on the fourth weekday, after the sixth hour to Bethlehem to celebrate the vigils, for the vigils are kept in Bethlehem, in the church wherein is the cave [1] where the Lord was born)—On this fifth weekday, the fortieth day after Easter, the dismissal [2] is celebrated in its due order, so that the priests and the bishop preach, treating of the things suitable to the day and the place, and afterwards every one returns to Jerusalem late.

VI

Festivals of Whitsuntide

1. *Whitsunday.*—(*a*) *Morning Station.*[3]

But on the fiftieth day, that is, the Lord's Day, when the people have a very great deal to go through, everything that is customary is done from the first

---

canon is performed : Ps. xcvii.[6]; Epistle of Cyril, bishop of Jerusalem to Constantine; Gal. vi. 14–18; Alleluiah; Ps. xcviii.; S. Matt. xxiv. 30–35."

[1] See Introduction, p. xlvii.

[2] Lat. *missa celebratur.*

[3] In the Old Arm. Lect. we have as follows: "On the Sunday of Holy Pentecost, they assemble in the holy Shrine. Canon: Ps. cxliii.[10]; Acts ii. 1–21; Alleluiah; Ps. How lovely are the courts; S. John xiv. 15–24.

At the same time, after the dismissal from the Shrine at the third hour, they proceed to holy Sion. Canon: Ps. the same, and same lection; S. John xiv. 25-29.

On the same Sunday, at the tenth hour, they assemble on the holy Mount of Olives, and the same Psalm and the same lection are used, S. John xvi. 5–15. And there, after the Gospel, takes place a *gonuklisia*, thrice. And in all places in the same manner, and at even they proceed to Holy Sion. Canon: Ps. cxliii. 10; S. John xiv. 15–24."

cockcrow onwards; vigil is kept in the Anastasis, and the bishop reads the passage from the Gospel that is always read on the Lord's Day, namely, the account of the Lord's Resurrection, and afterwards everything customary is done in the Anastasis, just as throughout the whole year. But when morning is come, all the people proceed to the great church, that is, to the martyrium, and all things usual are done there; the priests preach and then the bishop, and all things that are prescribed are done, the oblation being made, as is customary on the Lord's Day, only the same dismissal [1] in the martyrium is hastened, in order that it may be made before the third hour.

(b) *Station at Sion.*

And when the dismissal has been made at the martyrium, all the people, to a man, escort the bishop with hymns to Sion, [so that] they are in Sion when the third hour is fully come. And on their arrival there the passage from the Acts of the Apostles [2] is read where the Spirit came down so that all tongues [were heard and all men] understood the things that were being spoken, and the dismissal takes place afterwards in due course. For the priests read there from the Acts of the Apostles concerning the selfsame thing, because that is the place in Sion—there is another church there now—where once, after the Lord's Passion, the multitude was gathered together with the Apostles,

---

[1] Lat. *eadem adceleratur missa.*
[2] Acts ii. 1 ff.

THE PILGRIMAGE OF ETHERIA 87

and where this was done, as we have said above. Afterwards the dismissal takes place in due course, and the oblation is made there. Then, that the people may be dismissed, the archdeacon raises his voice, and says: "Let us all be ready to-day in Eleona, in the Imbomon, directly after the sixth hour."

(c) *Station at the Mount of Olives.*

So all the people return, each to his house, to rest themselves, and immediately after breakfast they ascend the Mount of Olives, that is, to Eleona, each as he can, so that there is no Christian left in the city who does not go. When, therefore, they have gone up the Mount of Olives, that is, to Eleona, they first enter the Imbomon, that is, the place whence the Lord ascended into heaven, and the bishops and the priests take their seat there, and likewise all the people. Lessons are read there with hymns interspersed, antiphons too are said suitable to the day and the place, also the prayers which are interspersed have likewise similar references. The passage from the Gospel is also read where it speaks of the Lord's Ascension, also that from the Acts of the Apostles[1] which tells of the Ascension of the Lord into heaven after His Resurrection. And when this is over, the catechumens and then the faithful are blessed, and they come down thence, it being already the ninth hour, and go with hymns to that church which is in Eleona, wherein is the cave where the Lord was wont to sit and teach His Apostles. And as it is already

[1] S. Luke xxiv 50 ff.; Acts i. 9 ff.

past the tenth hour when they arrive, *lucernare* takes place there; prayer is made, and the catechumens and likewise the faithful are blessed.

(*d*) *Night Procession.*

And then all the people to a man descend thence with the bishop, saying hymns and antiphons suitable to that day, and so come very slowly to the martyrium. It is already night when they reach the gate of the city, and about two hundred church candles are provided for the use of the people. And as it is a good distance from the gate to the great church, that is, the martyrium, they arrive about the second hour of the night, for they go the whole way very slowly lest the people should be weary from being afoot. And when the great gates are opened, which face towards the market-place, all the people enter the martyrium with hymns and with the bishop. And when they have entered the church, hymns are said, prayer is made, the catechumens and also the faithful are blessed; after which they go again with hymns to the Anastasis, where on their arrival hymns and antiphons are said, prayer is made, the catechumens and also the faithful are blessed; this is likewise done at the Cross. Lastly, all the Christian people to a man escort the bishop with hymns to Sion, and when they are come there, suitable lessons are read, psalms and antiphons are said, prayer is made, the catechumens and the faithful are blessed, and the dismissal takes place. And after the dismissal all approach the bishop's hand, and then every one returns to his house about midnight.

Thus very great fatigue is endured on that day, for vigil is kept at the Anastasis from the first cockcrow, and there is no pause from that time onward throughout the whole day, but the whole celebration (of the Feast) lasts so long that it is midnight when every one returns home after the dismissal has taken place at Sion.

2. *Resumption of the Ordinary Services.*

Now, from the day after the fiftieth day all fast as is customary throughout the whole year, each one as he is able, except on the Sabbath and on the Lord's Day, which are never kept as fasts in this place. On the ensuing days everything is done as during the whole year, that is, vigil is kept in the Anastasis from the first cockcrow. And if it be the Lord's Day, at the earliest cockcrow the bishop first reads in the Anastasis, as is customary, the passage from the Gospel concerning the Resurrection, which is always read on the Lord's Day, and then afterwards hymns and antiphons are said in the Anastasis until daylight. But if it be not the Lord's Day, only hymns and antiphons are said in like manner in the Anastasis from the first cockcrow until daylight. All the *apotactitae*, and of the people those who are able, attend ; the clergy go by turns, daily. The clergy go there at first cockcrow, but the bishop always as it begins to dawn, that the morning dismissal may be made with all the clergy present except on the Lord's Day, when (the bishop) has to go at the first cockcrow, that he may read the Gospel in the Anastasis. Afterwards everything is done as usual in the Anastasis until the sixth hour, and at the ninth, as well as at *lucernare*, according to the custom of the whole year. But on the fourth and sixth weekdays, the ninth hour is kept in Sion as is customary.

VII

BAPTISM [1]

1. *The Inscribing of the Competents.*

Moreover, I must write how they are taught who are baptised at Easter. Now he who gives in his name, gives it in on the day before Quadragesima, and the priest writes down the names of all; this is before the eight weeks which I have said are kept here at Quadragesima. And when the priest has written down the names of all, after the next day of Quadragesima, that is, on the day when the eight weeks begin, the chair is set for the bishop in the midst of the great church, that is, at the martyrium, and the priests sit in chairs on either side of him, while all the clergy stand. Then one by one the competents are brought up, coming, if they are males (*viri*) with their fathers, and if females (*feminae*), with their mothers. Then the bishop asks the neighbours of every one who has entered concerning each individual, saying: "Does this person lead a good life, is he obedient to his parents, is he not given to wine, nor deceitful?" making also inquiry about the several vices which are more serious in man.[2] And if he

---

[1] For this section see Thompson on *Baptismal Offices*, pp. 52 ff.
[2] Lat. *singula vitia quae sunt tamen graviora in homine.* It is difficult to decide whether this means "the various more

has proved him in the presence of witnesses to be blameless in all these matters concerning which he has made inquiry, he writes down his name with his own hand. But if he is accused in any matter, he orders him to go out, saying: "Let him amend, and when he has amended then let him come to the font (*lavacrum*)." And as he makes inquiry concerning the men, so also does he concerning the women. But if any be a stranger, he comes not so easily to Baptism, unless he has testimonials from those who know him.

2. *Preparation for Baptism—Catechisings.*

This also I must write, reverend sisters, lest you should think that these things are done without good reason. The custom here is that they who come to Baptism through those forty days, which are kept as fast days, are first exorcised by the clergy early in the day, as soon as the morning dismissal has been made in the Anastasis. Immediately afterwards the chair is placed for the bishop at the martyrium in the great church, and all who are to be baptised sit around, near the bishop, both men and women, their fathers and mothers standing there also. Besides these, all the people who wish to hear come in and sit down—the faithful however only, for no catechumen enters there when the bishop teaches the others the Law. Beginning from Genesis he goes through all the Scriptures

---

serious human vices" (in males and females), in which case there is apparently no force in *tamen*, or "the various vices, which are more serious in a male (than in a female) all the same," in which case Etheria uses *homo*, where just before and after she uses *vir*.

during those forty days, explaining them, first literally, and then unfolding them spiritually. They are also taught about the Resurrection, and likewise all things concerning the Faith during those days. And this is called the catechising.

3. "*Traditio*" *of the Creed.*

Then when five weeks are completed from the time when their teaching began, (the Competents) are then taught the Creed.[1] And as he explained the meaning of all the Scriptures, so does he explain the meaning of the Creed; each article first literally and then spiritually. By this means all the faithful in these parts follow the Scriptures when they are read in church, inasmuch as they are all taught during those forty days from the first to the third hour, for the catechising lasts for three hours. And God knows, reverend sisters, that the voices of the faithful who come in to hear the catechising are louder (in approval) of the things spoken and explained by the bishop than they are when he sits and preaches in church. Then, after the dismissal of the catechising is made, it being already the third hour, the bishop is at once escorted with hymns to the Anastasis. So the dismissal takes place at the third hour. Thus are they taught for three hours a day for seven weeks, but in the eighth week of Quadragesima, which is called the Great Week, there is no time for them to be taught, because the things that are [described] above must be carried out.[2]

---

[1] Lat. *accipient simbolum.*
[2] *i.e.* the Holy Week Services.

4. "*Redditio*" [*Recitation*] *of the Creed.*

And when the seven weeks are past, [and] the Paschal week is left, which they call here the Great Week, then the bishop comes in the morning into the great church at the martyrium, and the chair is placed for him in the apse behind the altar, where they come one by one, a man with his father and a woman with her mother, and recite the Creed to the bishop. And when they have recited the Creed to the bishop, he addresses them all, and says: "During these seven weeks you have been taught all the law of the Scriptures, you have also heard concerning the Faith, and concerning the resurrection of the flesh, and the whole meaning of the Creed, as far as you were able, being yet catechumens. But the teachings of the deeper mystery, that is, of Baptism itself, you cannot hear, being as yet catechumens. But, lest you should think that anything is done without good reason, these, when you have been baptised in the Name of God, you shall hear in the Anastasis, during the eight Paschal days, after the dismissal from the church has been made. You, being as yet catechumens, cannot be told the more secret mysteries of God."

5. *Mystic Catechisings.*

But when the days of Easter have come, during those eight days, that is, from Easter to the Octave, when the dismissal from the church has been made, they go with hymns to the Anastasis. Prayer is said anon, the faithful are blessed, and the bishop stands, leaning against the inner rails which are in the cave of the Anastasis, and explains all things that are done in Baptism. In that hour no catechumen approaches the Anastasis, but only the neophytes and the faithful, who wish to hear concerning the mysteries, enter there, and the doors are shut lest any catechumen should draw near. And while the bishop discusses and sets forth each point, the voices of those who applaud are so loud that they can be heard outside the church. And truly the mysteries are so unfolded that there is no one unmoved at the things that he hears to be so explained.

Now, forasmuch as in that province some of the people know both Greek and Syriac, while some know Greek alone and others only Syriac; and because the bishop, although he knows Syriac, yet always speaks Greek, and never Syriac, there is always a priest standing by who, when the bishop speaks Greek, interprets into Syriac, that all may understand what is being taught. And because all the lessons that are read in the church must be read in Greek, he always stands by and interprets them into Syriac, for the people's sake, that they may always be edified. Moreover, the Latins here, who understand neither Syriac nor Greek, in order that they be not disappointed, have (all things) explained to them, for there are other brothers and sisters knowing both Greek and Latin, who translate into Latin for them. But what is above all things very pleasant and admirable here, is that the hymns, the antiphons, and the lessons, as well as the prayers which the bishop says, always have suitable and fitting references, both to the day that is being celebrated and also to the place where the celebration is taking place.

VIII

DEDICATION OF CHURCHES[1]

Those are called the days of dedication when the holy church which is in Golgotha, and which they call the martyrium, was consecrated to God; the holy church also which is at the Anastasis, that is, in the place where the Lord rose after His Passion, was consecrated to God on that day. The dedication of these holy churches is therefore celebrated with the highest honour, because the Cross of the Lord was found on this same day. And it was so ordained that, when the holy churches above mentioned were first consecrated, that should be the day when the Cross of the Lord had been found, in order that the whole celebration should be made together, with all rejoicing, on the self-same day. Moreover, it appears from the Holy Scriptures[2] that this is also the day of dedication, when holy Solomon, having finished the House of God which he had built, stood before the altar of God and prayed, as it is written in the books of the Chronicles.

So when these days of dedication are come, they are kept for eight days. And people begin to assemble from all parts many days before; not only monks

---

[1] In the Old Arm. Lect. we have: "September 23, dedication of the holy places. On the first day in the holy Anastasis, this canon is performed: Ps. lxv.[1]; Tim. iii. 14-16; Alleluiah: Ps. cxlvii.[12]; S. John x. 22-42 . . ." [Mr. Conybeare notes that in the MS. the last line of this lection is torn away as well as the beginning of the rubric which follows, and which related to the feast of the Cross, called *Warag*, on the following day.]

[2] 2 Chron. vi., vii. 8-10.

and *apotactitae* from various provinces, from Mesopotamia and Syria, from Egypt and the Thebaid (where there are very many monks), and from every different place and province—for there is none who does not turn his steps to Jerusalem on that day for such rejoicing and for such high days—but lay people too in like manner, both men and women, with faithful minds, gather together in Jerusalem from every province on those days, for the sake of the holy day. And the bishops, even when they have been few, are present to the number of forty or fifty in Jerusalem on these days, and with them come many of their clergy. But why should I say more? for he who on these days has not been present at so solemn a feast thinks that he has committed a very great sin, unless some necessity, which keeps a man back from carrying out a good resolution, has hindered him. Now on these days of the dedication the adornment of all the churches is the same as at Easter and at Epiphany, also on each day the procession is made to the several holy places, as at Easter and at Epiphany. For on the first and second days it is to the greater church, which is called the martyrium. On the third day it is to Eleona, that is, the church which is on that mount whence the Lord ascended into heaven after His Passion, and in this church is the cave wherein the Lord used to teach His Apostles on the Mount of Olives. But on the fourth day . . .

INDEX OF PROPER NAMES AND THINGS

AARON, 7, 9, 16
Abgar, xxiv, 30 ff.
—— his likeness, xxiv, xlvii, 33
Abraham (Abram), xxxiii, xxxvii n., 26, 36 f.
—— his house, 36
Acta Thaddaei, xxxvi
Acts of Apostles. *See* Apostles
Acts of S. Thecla. *See* S. Thecla
Acts of S. Thomas. *See* S. Thomas
Adornment of Churches, xlvi, 53, 55, 80, 96
Aelia (Jerusalem), 18
Ænon, xxii, xliv, 27 f.
Agri specula, 24
Alexandria, xviii n., xix, xxvii n., 6, 18
—— patriarch of, xxvi
Amalek, xviii
Ambrose, S., xl, 75 n.
Amphilochius quoted, xxxii
Ananias the courier, 30, 33, 35
Anastasis, Church of, xlv, 45 ff.
Anastasius, Emperor, xiii
Anna the prophetess, xxxvii, 56
Anthony, rule of S., xxvii f.
Antioch, xviii, xxiii, xxv, xxxvii, 31, 41
—— patriarch of, xxvii
Antiphons, xxxix f., 28, 45 ff.
Apostles, Church of, xlvi, 44
—— Acts of, 86, 87
—— Epistles of, 76
Apostolic Constitutions quoted, xlii, xliii n.
Apotactitae, xxix, xlii, xlvii, 42, 43, 62, 82, 83, 89, 96

Arabia, 25
—— city of, xix, xx, 13, 16; its bishop, xx, xxx, 16, 17
—— mountains of, 19
Archdeacon, xliv f., 63, 65, 70, 87
Arianism, xl
Arles, ix, xvii
Armenia, Catholicos of, xxvii
Armenian Lectionary, xli, 52 n.
Ascension, Feast of, xxxviii f., xlvii, 84, 87
Ascetics, xii, xiii, xxvii ff., xxxvii, xxxix, 4, 21, 29, 37, 39
Asia, 44
Asses used, xii, 21
Astorga, viii
Athanasius, S., quoted, xlii
Augustine, S., quoted, xlii
Augustofratensis, province of, 31
Ausitis. *See* Uz

Baalzephon, xix, 14
Balaam, 24
Balak, 24
Balsam, 17
Baptism, xliii f., 90 ff.
Baptisms at Ænon, 27 f.
Bardesanes, xl
Bashan, xxxiv n., 24
Batiffol, Pierre, xiii
Bathnae, xxiii, xxiv, 32
—— Bishop of, xiii, 32
Belisarius, xiv
Bernard, Archbishop, vii, xiv, xvi, xx, xxiv, xxx, xxxviii, xxxix n., xli f., xlvi, 17 n., 21 n., 22 n., 25 n., 28 n., 32 n. 43 n., 46 n., 62 n.

INDEX OF PROPER NAMES AND THINGS

Betham-Edwards, Miss, quoted, xx f.
Bethany, 63 ff.
—— Church of, xlvii, 63 f.
Beth-haran. *See* Livias
Bethlehem, xxxviii, 52 f.
—— Church of, xlvii, 54
Bethnel, 38
Bigg, Canon, 21 *n.*
Bishop, Edmund, xliii
Bishop's hand, to approach the, xl, 46 *n.*
Bithynia, xxv, 43
Bordeaux, Pilgrim of, xvii, 70 *n.*
Braga, Bishop of, viii
Brightman, Canon, 5 *n.*
Bubastir, xix
Burning. *See* Taberah
—— Bush, xix, 2, 7 f.
Butler, Dom, xxix *n.*

Cabrol, Dom, vii, 46 *n.*
Cæsarea, Bishop of, xxvii
Camels used, xii, 12
Cancelli. *See* Rails
Canon of Scripture, meaning of, xxxii
Cappadocia, xxv, 43
Carneas, xiii *n.*, xxii, xxix, xliv, 25, 29
—— Bishop of, 29 f.
Carthage, Councils of, xlii, xliv
Cassian quoted, xxx
Catechizing, 91 ff
Catechumens, xli, xliii, 48, 67 ff., 90 ff.
Catherine, Convent of S., xix
Cells (*monasteria*), xxx, 4, 5, 7, 11, 21, 28, 29, 40, 42
Cereofala, 48, 54
Chalcedon, xxv, xliv, 43
Chaldees, 39
Charræ. *See* Haran
Chedorlaomer (Quodollagomor), xxxii, 26
Cherith (Corra), xxii, 29
Children. *See* Infantes
Choir boys, xliii, 47
"Christ our God," 31, 32, 43, 44
Christmas, Feast of, xxxvii

Chronicles, Books of, 95
Chrysostom, S., quoted, xl
—— Liturgy of, xix *n.*
Cicendelae, 54
Cilicia, xxv, 41, 42
Clysma (Suez), xi, xviii, xix, 12 f
Cœle-Syria, 31
Competentes, xliii f., 90 ff.
Confessor, xiii, 32, 36
Constantine, Emperor, xlvi f., 50, 52, 54
Constantinople, vii *n.*, xi *n.*, xvii, xxiii, xxv, xlvi, 43, 44
—— Churches of, xxvi, 42 *n.*, 44
Conybeare, F. C., xxxvii, xxxix *n.*, xli, 39 *n.*, 62 *n.*, 70 *n.*, 95 *n.*
Coptic Church, xlv
Corra. *See* Cherith
Corycus, xxv, 42
Cosmas Indicopleustes quoted, xxxvii
Credner on the Canon, xxxii
Creed, "Traditio" of, 92
—— "Redditio" of, 93
Cross, Adoration of, xxxviii, 74 f.
—— Discovery of, xlvi, 95
—— Exaltation of, xlvi
—— Title of, xlv, 75
Cyril, S., of Jerusalem, xliv, 82 *n.*, 85 *n.*
Cyrus, Bishop of Edessa, xxiv

Daily offices, xxxix, 45 ff.
Daphno. *See* Tahpanhes
Deaconess, xliv, 42
Dead Sea, 23, 24
Decian persecution, xxvii
Deconinck, Abbé, viii
Dedication, Feast of, xlvi, 95 f.
Dennaba, xxii, 25
Denzinger, H., xlv
Deuteronomy, Book of, xxxiii, 18, 19, 20
Dictionary of Bible, Hastings's, 17, 25, 41
—— *of Christian Biography*, xxiv, xxxvi, xl
—— *of Christian Antiquities*, xl
—— *of Prayer Book*, 50

INDEX OF PROPER NAMES AND THINGS

Diptychs, xliii, 47
Dowden, Bishop, xlii
Ducange quoted, 48 n.
Doctrina Apostolorum, xxxvi
—— *Addaei*, xxxvi
Duchesne, Monseigneur, viii, xiii, xv, xvi, xxvii, xxxvii, xxxviii, xlv, 46 n., 57 n., 63 n., 73 n., 84 n.

Easter, Feast of, xxxvii, xliv, 37, 49, 56, 80, 96
—— Vigil of, 78 f.
Edessa, xiv n., xxii, xxxvi, xliv
—— Bishop of, ix n., xiii, 32
—— new church of S. Thomas, xxiii, 32
—— Chronicle of, xxiii
Edom. *See* Idumæa
Edrei (Sasdra), 24
Egeria, viii n.
Egypt, xi, xii, xix, xxi, xxvi, xxxvii, 6, 10, 13, 17, 96
—— monks of, xxvii ff.
Eleona, xxxix, xlvii, 55 f.
Eliezer of Damascus, xxxiv, 36
Elijah, xviii, xxii, 6, 28
Elpidius. *See* Helpidius, S.
Eortae, name for Lent, xxxviii, 57
Epauleum (Pi-hahiroth), xix, 14
Ephesus, xxvi, xliv, 44
Ephraem Syrus, xxiv, xl
Epiphany, Feast of, xx, xxxvii, xlvii, 16, 52 ff., 96
Epiphanius quoted, xxx n.
Esebon (Exebon). *See* Heshbon
Etham, 14
Etheria, her date and country, viii ff.; her rank, xi; her language, ix f.; her knowledge of Greek, x, xxv, xlvii f.; her use of Scripture, xxxi ff.; her mode of travelling, xii; her route, xvii ff.; she receives Communion, 5, 30, 43; gives thanks, 28, 29, 30, 40, 43; her sisters in religion, 5, 10, 23, 31, 36, 37, 40, 44, 45, 91, 92
Eucharist, xlii f.
Eucheria, viii n.

Eulogiae, xlv, 5, 21, 28, 40
Eulogius, Bishop of Edessa, xiii, xxiv
Euphemia, S., tomb of, xxv, xliv, 43
Euphrates, xxiii, 31 f.
Eusebius the historian quoted, xxiv, xlvi f., 18 n., 30 n.
Evans, Canon Charles, xv
Exodus, route of, xix, 10

Fadana (Paddan-Aram), xxv, 41
Faran. *See* Paran
Fasting, rules for, xli f., 57, 61 f.
Férotin, Dom, vii f., xi n., xvii n.
Fogor. *See* Peor
Fructuosus, S., of Braga, viii

Gad, 19
Galatia, xxv, 43
Galla Placidia, vii n., xii
Gallaecia, viii, ix, xi n.
Gallia Narbonensis, ix
Gamurrini, Signor, vii, x, xxiv, 25 n., 62 n.
Gasquet, Abbé, xxix n.
Genesis, Book of, xxxiii, 15, 36, 40
Gerapolis. *See* Hierapolis
Getha, Tomb of, 28.
Gethsemane, xlvii, 71 f.
Geyer, M. Paul, vii
Gibson, Mrs., and Mrs. Lewis, quoted, 46 n.
Glory of God, and Glory of the Lord, 3 f.
Golgotha, xlv, 53 ff.
Good Friday observances, xxxviii, 73 f.
Graves of Lust. *See* Kibroth Hattaavah
Greek, use of, x, xxiv, xliii, xlvii f., 94
Gregory Asharuni, xli, 52 n., 59 n.
Gregory, S., of Tours, 54 n., 59 n.
Goshen, xix, xx, 13, 15
—— fertility of, xx f., 17

Haran (Charræ), xxv, xxix, xxxi, xliv, 36
——Bishop of, xiii, xxxvi, 36, 39

Heathen mentioned, 38
Helena, Empress, xlvii, 54
Helpidius (Elpidius), S., xxv, xxix, xliv, 37
Herbert, Rev. George, xv
Hermon, Mount, xxii
Heroopolis, xix, 15
Heshbon (Esebon), 23
Hierapolis (Gerapolis), xxiii, xxvii, 31
Hilarion, xxviii
Hilary of Poictiers, xxxvi
Hisauria. *See* Isauria
Holy Week observances, xxxviii, 63 ff.
Horeb, Mount, xviii, 6
Horn, for anointing kings, xxxviii, 75
Hur. *See* Ur
Hymns, xxxix f., 45 ff.

Idumaea (Edom), 24, 25
Imbomon, xxxviii, xlvii, 66 ff.
Incense, xliii, 49
Infantes (children or the baptized), 66, 79, 82. *See* also *Neophyti*
Isaac, 38
Isauria, xxv, xxix, xliv, 41, 42, 43
Israelites, 13, 16, 20, 24

Jacob, xxv, 15, 39, 41
Jebel el Deir, xviii *n*.
Jebel Musa, xviii
Jericho, xxi f., 19, 23, 24
Jerome, S., quoted, xxxiv, xxxvi
Jerusalem, xii, xviii, xxii, xxix, xxxvii, xl f., xliv, xlvi, 18, 19, 24, 30, 31, 41
—— churches of, xiv, xlv
—— Bishop of, xxvii, 45 ff.; his house, xlvi, 50
—— services in, 45 ff.
"Jesus our God," 18, 30, 36
Job, xxii, 24 ff.
—— grave of, xliv, 29
John, S., tomb of, xxvi, xliv, 44
John the Baptist, S., xliv, xlv, 27 f.
Jordan, xxi f., xxvii, xxix, 19, 28
Joseph, son of Jacob, 15

Joseph of Arimathæa, 77
—— of Nazareth, S., 56
Joshua, 9, 19
—— book of, 19
Jovian, Emperor, xiv, 39 *n*.
Judges, Book of, 28
Justinian, Emperor, ix, xiv, 42 *n*.
Juvenal, Bishop of Jerusalem, xxxvii

Kibroth Hattaavah (Graves of Lust), xvii, 1, 11
Kings, Book of, 7
—— *See* Horn
Köhler, vii *n*.
Kyrie Eleison, xliii, 47

Laban, 39, 41
Laodicea, Council of, xlii
Lay people (*laici, sæculares*), xxx *n*., 45, 56, 96
Lazarium, xlvii, 55, 63 f., 80
Lazarus, sister of, xlvii, 64
Lent, observances of, 57 ff.
—— duration of, xxxviii
—— fast of, xxviii *n*., xli f., 59, 61 f.
Livias (Beth-haran), xxi, 19, 20, 23
Lord's Day, 49 ff., 57 f.
Lot's wife, 23
Lowther-Clarke, Rev. W. K., xxvii *n*., xxviii *n*.
Lucernae, 54
Lucernare (*licinicon*, vespers), xxxix, 28, 47 ff.

Magnus (Ma'nû), xxiv, 33
Manasseh, 19
Manichaeans, xxx
Mansocrenae. *See* Mopsocrene
Ma'nû. *See* Magnus
Marseilles, ix
Marthana (the deaconess), xxv, xxix, xliv, 42
Martyrology, Syriac, 37 *n*., 42 *n*., 43 *n*.
Martyrs' memorials, xliv
—— days in Lent, xlii, 59
Mary of Bethany. *See* Lazarus

INDEX OF PROPER NAMES AND THINGS

Mas'oudy, the traveller, quoted, xx
Mattins, xxxix, 45 f.
Maundy Thursday observances, xxxviii, xlii, 69 f.
Mediterranean Sea, xvi n., 6
Meister, Karl, viii ff., xiii ff., xxi, xxiv
Melchizedek, xxii, xxxiv, xliv, xlviii, 25 ff.
Mesopotamia, xiii, xxii, xxvii, xxxvii, 30, 32 37, 96
Migdol, xix, 14
Milan, xl, xliii, 54 n.
Missa, meaning of, xl f.
Moab, xxi, xxxiv, 18 f.
Monazontes, xxix, 45
Monks, viii, xxvii ff.
—— as cultivators, xxxi, 5, 28
Mopsocrene (Mansocrenae), xxv, 43
Moses, xviii, xxii, xxxi, xxxiv, 2, 4, 5, 7, 8, 9, 11, 16, 20, 21, 24
—— books of, xxxi, 5, 7, 8, 16, 19, 21, 22, 26
Mules, xii
Mysteries, instruction about, 93 f.

Nahor, 38
Naville, Ed., xx n.
Nebo, Mount, xi, xii, xxi, xlv, 18, 20, 22
Neophytes, 94. *See* also Infantes
Nicæa, Council of, xxvii
Nile, xix, 15, 17
Nisibis, xiii, xxv, 39
Nitria, xxvii n.
None, xxxix, 46
Nuns, xi n., xxvii ff., 42, 45 ff.

Oblatio, xix, xxii, xli, 5, 7, 11, 30, 60, 70, 76, 80, 86
Officers, Roman, 14
Og, King of Bashan, 24
Origen quoted, xxxiii
Osrhoene, xxiii, 32 n.
Ostraca, Coptic and Greek, x n., 10 n.

Pachomius, S., Rule of, xxvii f.

Paddan-Aram. *See* Fadana
Palladius, Lausiac History of, xii, xxv n.
Palm Sunday observances, xxxviii, 64 ff.
Palestine, monks of, xxviii f.
—— seen from Mount Sinai, 6
Paran (Faran), xii, xviii, xxii, 2, 11 ff.
Parthenae (virgins), xxix, 42, 45 ff.
Parthenian Sea, xviii n. 6
Passover, 10, 15
Paschal candle, 78 n.
Paul, S., connected with S. Thecla, xxxvi
Pelusium, xx, xxi, xxvi, 17, 18
Pentecost, festival of, xxxix, 85 ff.
—— fast after, xlii, 89
Peor (Fogor), 24
Persians, xxv, 33 f., 39
Peter the Deacon, xvii n.
Petrie, Prof. Flinders, xvi, 12
Pharaoh, 16, 17
Phœnicia, xxii, 29
Pilate, 77
Pithom, xix, 15
Pompeiopolis (Soli), xxv, 42
Prayers offered, 4, 7.
Provence, xliii
Prudentius, xl n.
Psalter, use of, xxxix, 45 ff.
Pseudo-Basil of Seleucia, xxix n.
Purification (Hypopaute), Feast of, xxxvii, 56

Quadragesimae, xxxviii, 57
Quodollagomor. *See* Chedorlaomer

Rachel's well, xxv, xxxi, 39, 40, 41
Rails (*cancelli*), 46 ff.
Rameses, xix, xx, 13, 15 f., 18
Rebecca, 36, 38
Red Sea, 6, 13 f.
Reuben, 19
Rhone, ix, xvii, 31
Rigby, Rev. A. D., xvi, xxxiv n.

INDEX OF PROPER NAMES AND THINGS

Ring of King Solomon, xxxviii, 75
Rituale Armenorum, xxxvii, 62 n.
Robbers, xxxi, 43; cf. 75
Roman Empire, borders of, xxxv, 39.
Rufianense monasterium, viii
Rufinus, the Imperial minister, vii
———, the writer, quoted, xxiv, 75 n.

Saft-el-Henneh, xx
Saints, lives of, xxxvi f.
Salem (Salim, Sedima), xxii, xxxiv, 25, 27
Sapor, King, xiv, 39 n.
Saracens, 6, 15
Sarah, 38
Sasdra. *See* Edrei
Sayce, Professor, 46 n.
Scete, xxvii n.
Scriptures, 1, 2, 11, 14, 16, 23, 31, 38, 51, 91
——— of the Canon, 38; of GOD, 39, 46
Sedima. *See* Salem
Segor. *See* Zoar
Seleucia, xviii n., xxix, xxxi, xxxvi, xliv, 42
Seon. *See* Sihon
Septuagint, readings of, xxxii ff., 18, 19
Sermons, xliii, 51, 56, 85
Sext, xxxix, 46
Sihon (Seon), King of Amorites, 23
Silvia, S., of Aquitaine, vii, viii, ix n., xii
Sinai, xi, xii, xiii, xvii, xxix, xxx, xliv, xlv, 1, 3, 10, 18
Sion, xlv, 52 ff.
Socrates, the historian, quoted, xxiii
Sodom, 23, 26
Soldiers, Roman, xi, xiv, xix, xx, 14, 17, 31
Soloman, King. *See* Ring; Temple
Sozomen, the historian, quoted, xlvi n.
Spain, viii, 78 n.

Spanish dialect, ix, x n.
Statuta ecclesiae antiqua, xliv
Succoth, xix, 14
Suez. *See* Clysma
Sychar, xxxiv
Sycomore tree, xx, 16
Symeon and Anna, xxxvii, 56
Syria, xxiii, 30, 96
———, Church of, xxvii, xlv
———, monks of, xxviii f.
Syriac, use of, x, xl, xliii
———, interpreter of, xliii, 94

Tabor, xxii f.
Taberah (Burning), xix, 10
Tabernacle, 11
Tahpanhes (Taphnis, Daphno) xxi, 17 n.
Taphnis. *See* Tahpanhes
Tarsus, xviii n., xxv, 41 ff.
Tatnis. *See* Zoan
Taurus, Mount, xxv, 43
Temple, Solomon, xlvi, 95
Terah, 38
Terce, xxxix, 58 f.
Tertullian quoted, xxxiii, xxxvi
Thaddaeus, xxxvi
Thebaid, xviii n., xix, xxxi, 17, 18, 96
Theban stone, xx, 16
Thecla, S., memorial of, xxv, xxix n., xliv, 41 ff.
———, Acts of, xxxvi, 43
Theodoret quoted, xxix n.
Theodosius, Emperor, vii, viii, xi n., xxx n..
———, the pilgrim, xiv
Thesbe (Thisbe), xxii, xxix, 28
Thomas, S., Apostle, xxiii, xxxvi, xliv, 30, 32, 85
———, Acts of, xxxvi
Thou, xix
Tribune of soldiers, xiv n., xxii, 30, 32
Three Hours, observance of, xxxviii, 76

Ur of the Chaldees (Hur), xiii, xxv, 39
Uz (Ausitis), xxii, 24

INDEX OF PROPER NAMES AND THINGS

Vaison, Council of, xlii.
Valens, Emperor, xiii, xxiii
Valerius, letter of, vii, xi *n.*, xii *n.*, xix *n.*, xx *n.*, xxii, xxvi *n.*
Vespers. *See Lucernare*
Vierzo, viii
Vigiliae nocturnae, xxxix, 45, 49
Virgin Mary, 56
Virgins. See *Parthenae*, Nuns

Vulgate, readings of, xxxii ff.

Westcott, Bishop, xxxi f.
Whitsuntide. *See* Pentecost
Wilson, Sir Charles W., vii, xviii, xix *n.*, 70 *n.*

Zoan (Tatnis, Tanis), xxi, xxxiv, 17 f.
Zoar (Segor), 23

www.ingramcontent.com/pod-product-compliance
Lightning Source LLC
Chambersburg PA
CBHW070911160426
43193CB00011B/1424